Alive and Why

Testimony Poetry

©2018 Adam J. Bodnar
All rights reserved.

ISBN-13: 978-1983546549
ISBN-10: 1983546542

CONTENT

FOREWORD - - - - - - 5

Stage 1: MARTYR MATERIAL - - - 6

    just on the cusp - - - - 7

    oh my creative Creator - - - 8

    hello end of her beginning - - - 10

    global warning - - - - 13

    up to a point - - - - - 14

    holy hooky - - - - - 16

    Fatherly Spotter - - - - 17

    a request for repentance in rest - - 19

    Dear Glamour - - - - 21

    the ethics of optics - - - - 22

    any time entertainment - - - 24

    promises post-promiscuity - - - 26

    aching for the forsaking - - - 28

    in lieu of the lure - - - - 30

    afternoon mission tripping up - - - 32

    ego on the altar - - - - 35

    the line drawn - - - - 37

    God's best friend - - - - 39

    militianaries - - - - - 41

Stage 2: THANKS FOR NOT STONING ME   -   43

    b.c.   -   -   -   -   -   -   44

    gratitude for the taken for granted   -   -   49

    crosscheck   -   -   -   -   -   51

    the turning   -   -   -   -   -   52

    nearing the ending   -   -   -   -   55

    long lost   -   -   -   -   -   58

    better than bacteria   -   -   -   -   60

    everyday backwards ballet   -   -   -   65

    God's hats   -   -   -   -   -   68

    the great play   -   -   -   -   -   71

    sentenced to freedom   -   -   -   -   73

    the fearful wonderful   -   -   -   -   78

    a picture of forever   -   -   -   -   81

Stage 3: EVEN IN WAR, I AM AT PEACE	83
pickup lines	84
the linchpin	87
Son of Maggot	90
connecting dots	92
J.O.Y.	98
vows for now	101
in remembrance	103
the appraisal	106
cement to be	111
all but One	113
traps	115
the chief of sins	118
Pharisaical disbelief	122
to Oslo (the dwarf hotot)	124
an only	126
at peace in war	127
unintentionability	129
this blessed test	131
The Most Cool	134
ABOUT ME	138

FOREWORD

My sincerest thanks goes out to everyone who ever suggested I get published and for anyone who has ever sat through any poem(s) of mine. It has taken me about seven and a half years to amass a collection and the inspiration sufficient for putting this book together. A huge and special thanks is due to my older brother, Jason, for especially encouraging me and always believing in me.

As you read, know that most if not all of the following poems were initially written for the purpose of being shared out loud and they were written with the thought that they might be the first and only poem some might ever hear of mine. This could account for some redundancy as well as my occasionally heavy use of rhyme and alliteration. They are also pretty much in the order which I wrote them, oldest first and beginning with the first poem I wrote since being a Christian. By now, I wouldn't consider all of the oldest poems to be 100% theologically sound. But rather than change them for this book, I thought they'd serve their purpose better by staying as they are in order to capture my thought process at that time. Most were written during spurts of creativity and some were written over the course of several months and with perhaps several months in between. That all said, the following poems have largely recorded the course of my faith so far since April 12th, 2010.

Thank you for reading and I hope what follows is received well by you.

Stage 1

MARTYR MATERIAL

just on the cusp

born bearing the cross of a chasm
this insatiable hole
no matter how much stuff gets stuffed in
it always wants more
even with all of whatever in this world
satisfy every need ten times over
put as much into the hole as it will hold
and still, it's nowhere near filled

it just grows
and as it does, it grows harder to feel full
for a depraved day at most
oh, but there must be a way
with just enough money, sex and drugs

but no
it just grows
and right when you think you find something or someone
good and genuine
that thing or person falls
far short and fast from perfection

so, you move on
trading it or them in
continuing the thirsty search
seeking anything but the Truth
the Truth they make ridiculous
the Truth they lead us to resist
the Truth that we are built to embrace

so squirm and writhe and twist
until you too find that nothing earthly ever fits
not even close
because that hole is and always was in the shape of a cross

oh my creative Creator

the greatest artist has everything for a canvas
and before we're even painted into a time and space
He fits us as the bristles of his brushes
so we could paint too
with ourselves
with the things we do
and all we have to do is move
with His instruction
with and as everything goes
in the same direction
such beautiful brush strokes
with different but the same colors
all adding up to the brightest light
the way, the truth and the life

but some bristles get lost
not knowing that they are made for this
they fall out
and some get swept back up again
remembering all that they've missed
or maybe for the first time since
either way, it is glorious
being so at peace with the universe
and being able to say it all makes sense

but some of the lost never return
and this upsets
thinking so highly of themselves
students to anything else
destroying His work
with paint-bombs and rollers
wrecking balls and jealous censors
they think of Him as a joke
while killing off so much of His living art
and pushing Him nearly to the brink
but however bad things get
it all leads to Him making it all right
eventually sending a certain someone back

and when we're spent
we'll have forever to paint
in heaven
if only we believe in Him
and maybe resist some distasteful temptation
but that's really only a suggestion
to appease the piece of Him within
because even in the end
just ask, and you're forgiven
and yes
for each and every one of us
He broke off a little piece of Himself
making us all potential artists
if only we could be entertained enough by the silence
and if only we would listen to our conscience
because that's Him
speaking to us
always with the good intention
always pulling in the same direction
closer and closer to Him

hello end of her beginning

this is not goodbye
starting with "over-protective"
this is only a time to redefine
and this is an invitation to really live
in every way
on and in
so go while you stay
guiding and guarding
and be missed while never gone
and let's get lost once again
you pick the direction
and let's get lost everywhere I go
everywhere we've been
cause to my effect
mother to my self
finally freed from need
and easily finding peace
in His mysterious ways
you've just been released
from that bodily prison
set free into the best place
the kingdom of heaven

and scouring the wrinkles
find the grey housing a few favorites
carved by closeness
and barely blurred by the millions of menial minutes
after lining our pockets with the scarce and precious

ah, the innocent careless
so concerned only with wondering and wandering
while always wanting to be older
and if and when we are
already with a few close-calls, scares and scars
we look back just for a second
each now slipping by a little faster
and still having and wanting to look forward
though not sure of what for
responsibilities and experiences?
some sense of control?
until someday we find ourselves old

God willing

and looking with no turning back
oh, how stupid we were
but that was some real fun we had, huh?

cooking with me in the other arm
feeding and raising
a little me and an able you play "joop"
pushing pediatric acrobatics to its limits
and narrowly escaping an early end
while sparing me school lunches and the bus ride
you drive and we wave to "our friend"
and we get lost
exploring and exciting the boring
we see and wonder about "the ghost"
and we mock and endure and celebrate the situation
we're like a cartoon or a comic strip
with our repertoire of catch phrases and inside jokes
"do widzenia i kup sobie trąbkę do pierdzenia"
we are each other's sidekick
but eventually you care for me more than I care for
and I get worse before I get better
but you are always awesome
mother

this is not goodbye
we will get lost again
in due time
when He takes me by the hand
to meet you there in heaven

global warning

siblings please
mind the signs of these endtimes
and know
there's no greater honor
and there's no better way to go
than the way of a modern martyr
so prepare to thank your killer
with this something to die for
he'll only be doing you a favor
so offer up that worthless flesh
as a sheep to the slaughter
and with a smile, face death
knowing where you're going for the longest while

and while they might have the guns and tasers
gas masks and chambers
we have the love and forgiveness
eternal life and Jesus
and they are just jealous
because all their money and power
they work so hard stressing over
lying so much and killing so many for
it doesn't buy bliss
only more and more emptiness

so let's give the devil our condolences
as we destroy his evil ways
with caring and kindness

and when we're faced with the ultimate test
we will say yes
I believe
and you can kill me, if you must
because whenever I go, I will be happy
having lived and dying for Him who died for us

up to a point

eye to eye and all ears
until the upsetting was said
something just too hard to accept
even though it is only one more step
thought absurd because of what was brought
the anything but

please, not vulnerability
please, not a willingness to change and its admitting
how could you even ask that of me?

well then, forget I said anything
and go on thinking whatever it is that keeps you sleeping
or
come to know
the path to life is often narrow
while the widest and most traveled might get you killed
and do or die says the time
not on our side
ticking away to see what we'll say
when asked the questions that bind

will you deny until death?
or live to accept?
all truth
in the forefront of wiser minds
where and as it is kept

and

if yes
then, will you hide?
or will you rise?
to share and shine
even in the place called complacency
where everything is as it seems
and the only thing for sure is that it's comfy
permitting entry to only half of the story
and placing the greatest precedent upon entertainment
never entertaining that or this that's real and real heavy

we'll all die sometime

are you ready?

holy hooky

claiming the Christian affliction
and exhibiting not a single righteous symptom
but the tests will be run just the same
until post mortem

and in the patiently waiting room
waiting for the patient to come to
still sedated
anesthetized by the enemy's lies
but they'll fall apart and wear off in the light
just in time for the open-your-heart surgery
followed by the open-your-eyes and mind therapy
hopefully

no insurance?
no problem
this treatment is free
just don't say the condition was pre-existing
because if that were the case, there would be no need
just relax and take in the life-giving disease
communicable by example
and chronic to the nth degree

Fatherly Spotter

suppose this world were a gym
and life, an exercise regimen
then notice the not uncommon progression
it might start off pretty nice and easy
and He might seem pretty awesome
until you max out
and think He's nowhere to be found
then something gets pulled
or dislocated
or some other painful thing happens
really only awful upon first glance

but then comes the blaming until hating Him
denying for however long before thanking Him

so let's skip those middle-men of emotion
and get straight to the thanking for that "bad" thing
for whatever was denied, shaped
and where ever there was pain, grew strength
like a workout for the soul
so be glad that those spiritual muscles are sore
and next time, flex them
give hardship the scare

funny
strange and kind of 'haha'

how backwards it seems
but what would He have done?
go against the flow of things
and what are we to do?
the same
and however tempting it is to throw in the towel
let us rejoice in our sufferings
welcome the chances to rely more upon Him
and check ourselves when showered with blessings

and when stressed by some trial or test
as He's yelling, "C'mon, just a little more!"
rest in knowing
He's in control
He knows the weights you can handle
and this too shall pass
and when it does
you'll be capable of a few more metaphysical reps
just be sure to reflect and stretch

a request for repentance in rest

an eternity ago so recently
falling victim to the vacuum so voluntarily
and addicted to the instead of You
for all of the used
from the drugs for their jollies
to the women for their bodies
oh my God
I am sorry

You've had to watch
while so many of Your gifts went unopened
and I was putting all that poison in me
breathing in that pollution so willingly
and giving myself over and over again to Your enemy
again God
I am sorry

and now, I am haunted by what I formerly wanted
in the revisiting visions from the past
please, please take out this trash
the left-over sinful litter
these remainders only remind of a stranger
found as someone else when once so lost

but even after the losses were cut
still is the residue of his exploits

traces of the wanton desires
please extinguish these now tiniest of fires
for they still hurt and burn
their smoke stinks and chokes
and their lesson has been learned

there is nothing of value
not a hint of fulfillment
nothing but a gain-less pain
awaiting those trusting their gut
bound up by that faulty brain
and led astray by that deceitful heart

please, please cut these pictures out
don't place them into a scrapbook
just burn them up
up and away by the biggest flame
that which shouts, shoots and scrapes at the skies
with a warmth felt and a light seen for miles
all for You

please

thank You

Dear Glamour

with all due respect
please stop sending us your bio-hazardous magazine
no women live here
and it's clear
you're just a gear in the machine
grinding up the fairer gender
caught up in the world not-so blue and green
where reading is only feeding the cancer of one's self-esteem
because you take the liberty to standardize beauty
as if it has anything to do with exfoliating
and as if the best thing a person can be is sexy
but while in full pursuit of that or any lie
feel free to think of yourself as deep
because on the inside, you're below sea level by about six feet

sorry to pick on you specifically
there's plenty worse out there
sadly
you just happen to be responsible for our trash bags being so heavy
plus I think you're an adequate representation of the main-stream
seeing as you are just a smiley-face put to pornography
you and your cesspool's excuse for literature
of which I choose to not poison myself
because I can't even get past the cover
this being perhaps the most malicious issue ever
disguised by a few futile tips to live a fulfilling life
I wonder
have you ever tried Jesus Christ?

well, I'll be praying for you
and maybe you'll stop pushing your pollution sometime soon
but regardless, thank you for the inspiration
and to you and your models immodestly dressed
for which I might have once lusted
God bless

Sincerely,
disgusted

the ethics of optics

though it gives life
see how the light burns and blinds
it almost doesn't seem right
that darkness should be so easy on the eyes
and not hearing it like it is
so pleasing to the ears are the lies
speaking to that darkness within us
and this is the because of so many whys

crawling out from our cadaverous slumber
we wake like daytime vampires
rattled by how the brightness exposes
and merely speaking makes us liars
talking our ways out of wanting what we need
passing on the heavy but healthy
in favor of what with which we already agree
and taking in only what is tasty
for it is of the darkness that we feed
it is the darkness that allows us to sleep
we will come and go only to where it's comfy
because in the darkness, we ourselves keep

naturally
no one is taught these things
for it's the truth that hurts
it's the light that stings

now, if conformity were a crime
we would all stand guilty
a few of us, honorably
but the rest, not so much
sentenced to darkness is the overwhelming majority
for now confusing themselves for free
just prisoners in the darkness, where they choose to remain

but if it's the light that we seek
it is a light that we will be
and in a world so dark
it's not so easy
for it is the abstaining that stand out
because giving in has never been unique
and the only thing we're called to resist is instinct

any time entertainment

the most interesting movie ever isn't playing at your local theatre
it can't be rented, downloaded, bought or borrowed
because it's already yours and it's right here
and from your point of view, surely you're the star
hopefully you've got some decent supporting roles
but more importantly, good communication with the Director
because, like it or not, He calls the shots
but He might not seem to say much
you might even just wish He'd send you a text
but those who believe without seeing are blessed
and if His cues for you are missed
this will likely play out like some bad reality TV
as opposed to the epic tale that it could be
and every now and again He might throw in a plot twist
a new character makes an appearance
or maybe your romantic comedy turns into a tear-jerker
leaving you pissed and questioning whether He even exists
or you can take this chance for what it is
letting yourself grow into a stronger protagonist
sticking to the script
pressing on and giving thanks

you see, really nothing is meaningless
and if you're hearing this
this announcement
my public service

I pray that it encourages
to know that you have a purpose
a role to play in this world of a stage
not much like a channel you can change
or maybe reading like a novel book
every day, an un-promised page

or maybe this is like a game
if say, that's your poison
so in depth and with the greatest graphics
and you don't even need the latest system
nor a computer deemed this week, the fastest
just a pulse and a pair of eyes
see and realize
there are rules
and to every player, they apply
there's just no reset button
and only when it's game over can it be beaten
victory having less to do with how much you've tried
everything to do with your regard for the Lead Programmer

you know, the One for you, that died

for He who wrote the code is the One who scored
the impossibly highest of high scores
and He is willing to put your initials where His goes
and if He does, Him you'll know
and He is He who put into your hands your body of a controller
all that's needed to rack up the spiritual experience points

eventually moving on and up to the next level
where the big problems of yester-whenever seem so little
until you make it to that first and final boss
surprise, it's yourself with whom you'll wrestle
for what might feel like forever
but then comes the omniscient credits and a heavenly sort of sequel

promises post-promiscuity

oh thank God for that teenage awkwardness
for the keeping clean in a painful loneliness
for the keeping me from hurting any worse or anyone else

it's just too bad for that eventual confidence
the reflex to the trials and errors
the strike-outs
the sleep-overs
pursuing what my flesh wanted and the world encouraged
the getting into someone else's pants

this is for the purity I've stolen from future husbands
and one current, back then
for all the lies spoken that led hearts to be broken
for all the misled, led on and let down
this is for you
I have awoken
and I pray that you do too
as much as I didn't then
I'll admit it now
I used you
I got what I thought I wanted and moved on
unfulfilled, not unlike yourself

Dear God, tell me my callousness didn't rub off
I pray that they've learned the same as myself
please say my wrestling with this lesson was also their last

and although I desire each of their forgiveness
it takes only His to be cleansed
made anew
and now vowing to Him as well as a wife I might never have

my eyes will be starved
my thoughts will be held captive
and I will save all of my kisses and caresses
until that missed-before-she's-even-met Miss becomes my Misses

and maybe someday, her and I will have kids
but I'm getting ahead of myself
for that is all His business
and I am perfectly content with this
where and whenever this is
who and whatever He provides
and nothing else
because He knows best
and the sweetest dreams are made of this
not even looking for that one
but if He gives me to her and her to me
as I am now, and as I intend to be
not helping any more women get used to being used
the best of friends we will be before we marry
and only then will we be fused

aching for the forsaking

nothing kills me
like wondering how heavenly heaven's going to be
if it's missing so many
including most of my friends and so much of my family
aside from my mother, who's there for sure
I expect to meet strangers mostly
who are brothers and sisters really
but still
I'll miss dozens of those who I care about most
who I can't even talk to about this

and if I wouldn't be so busy basking in the infinite happiness
I just might be kicking myself
for not praying instead of playing those pointless games
for not reading the Book instead of this or that crap
for not planting and watering seeds instead of watching the devil's TV

but that was the old and lost me
executed so justly
resurrected with a blessing-me-to-this-day kind of testimony
and armed by, through and with Him to firmly place
upon my sleeve to show my thanks
and I am not sorry
for it is my duty to discomfort the comfortable many
those travelling so casually down the broad path
straight towards the permanent death

and not knowing or caring to change course
just laughing off the gift that never stops giving
the discovering one's true self through a life that never stops living

oh but how unimpressed this world is
as I was
with its magnificence

in spite of the countless miracles staring us all in the face
just to live the life I thought I would want
I denied my own eternal spirit
for the deadly sake of convenience
betting that all of this was just an accident
while thinking myself content

and so not
how could I be?
while convinced that there's no point
and who stood to benefit?
from my hopeless doubt
and from my ideas of God stuffed into a box
hid away in some closet
not worth a further thought
believing of Him only what I want
whatever lets me sleep at night

well, whatever let me sleep at night
kept me asleep during the day and corpse-like
for so long
until I was found when I found out
God is God
whether you believe in Him or not
and He loves you more than one could imagine
but He just might allow the snuffing of you or me out
at any moment
and I don't know about you, but what would I say to Him then?
when He asks why I deserve to be let in

well God, I don't
I'm as wretched as the next
but I trust what You've promised
You see me as Your Son
You see me as righteous
because I see You as You
the Three in One
the Creator
Love
Amen

in lieu of the lure

pushing the limits of His own influence
the King of Kings clearly prompted this
a decision that doesn't yet make sense
but to obey is to trust

patience

anything He doesn't directly cause, He still knows of and allows
and even the worst of these serves a purpose
for He has in store only the best for each of us

nevertheless, what's best might not be what each of us wants
and so
one can't help but sometimes hope His perfect mind changes
right when this jaunt almost seems too hard
and it is then that the enemy makes an appearance
aiming to foil the Lord's plans and spoil you like a child
the father of lies offers a number of effortless ways out
assuming you're easily befriended by the world

no thanks devil
I've been down that dead end road of yours
and I found every turn in your direction only made the hurting worse
now it's time that I live and grow by God's Word
as denying you in favor of Him ensures
what's true and good endures
as I should

but I don't
not always anyway
sometimes falling just short
with those sneaky sins slipping inside my thoughts
knowing what my flesh likes

but now I'll take two steps forward after taking that one back
no thanks again demon
I won't be selling out the blessings and grace given
you could offer me a lifetime full of the spoils of your rotten kingdom
and they would serve as no comparison
not to even a second's worth of what's waiting for me in heaven

almost enough to make suicide sound tempting
but no thanks again Satan
for the choice I've chosen has already got me eternally living
and this life, like anything else of Him is a gift
not one I'll ever waste or test
for I can find joy
in but not of this fallen world of yours
even in these evil days
because I dwell in hope and I'm always looking up

so Lucifer, get lost
I know my Master
and for me, He has paid the cost

afternoon mission tripping up

out and about in the open
playing the introvert
on this opportunity-filled day
with a mind to mind my own
while eavesdropping just the same

storming to and through the door of the store of coffee
a younger-than-me search-party of three brings with them a cloud of negativity
and after about a million moments
one by one they are exiting
the first, the rated-R instigator
though I don't think of it until later
one on one would be the best way to approach her
and share
but then joined by the others
conducting what sounds like a complaining convention

"I hate this weather"
"I think I'm coming down with something"
"did you hear what so-and-so said about me?"
"My classes are so stupid this semester"
"I can't even stand my family any more"
"My roommate only thinks of herself"
"I should've been born 40 years ago"
"I wish my boss would just disappear"

wow
that's takes me back
to my approaching bottom
maybe I should approach them
knowing what I know now
no
that'd be crazy
and they don't want to hear what I have to say

oh well
relocating

into my comfortable corner
with a fly's eye-view
I spy an older guy joined by another
and quickly they get to the quirky trading of disturbing quotes
taking on the traits of some idolized murderer of a character
and expressing their admirations for the most effective distractions
so passionate they are about the killer filler
their means of escape from what stares them in the face
at least when they're apparently scarcely away
from the stealing screen
what a waste

"have you played 'Soul Eater 6' yet?"
"you have to stab him like a hundred times"
"I'm going to kill you dead"
"'Cruciflyer' is way better"
"when you die, you have to fight your way out of hell"
"it's good to be evil"
"I'm a level 37 Angel-Slayer"
"the blood and guts look so real"

wow
I remember those days
that daze
surely I should say something to these guys
having been there as I was
hopelessly hypnotized
I must let them know there's more
but no
and though it pains
to not reach out to these old and lost boys
I can't seem to bring myself
and I must apologize
what a waste

and now, through the coffee shop window
the best window would pass by
as you were sitting alone outside
just shy from feeding the need
and looking so empty even with several wants within arms' reach
refined sugar for the eating
nicotine for breathing
and caffeine for the drinking
any more things of that vein would say those veins look bored

of what could she be thinking?

"life is such a chore"
"I got so drunk last night"
"this town sucks"
"why did I sleep with him?"
"I'm so ugly"
"why am I even here?"
"I'm almost out of cigarettes"
"I don't care anymore"

wow
now I've got to talk with her
this, I really must share
what's the worst that could happen?
oh, I don't know
wait, she's getting up
oh, it'd be too weird now
as she's walking to her car to continue
searching for that something
out of view
oh and here comes the grieving
so weak and disobedient
wait, why aren't you leaving?
maybe "something" is telling you to stay just a little longer
ample time for me to grow stronger

let me just run a scenario or two
and I'm weighed down by these excuses
pushing away that which pushes
and as my heart pulls, the rest of me refuses

epic fail
met with my inaction
just let so many chances slip away
oh well
it seems my lips are sealed by some devil

oh, ow
holding in this truth
still my cells strain to scream
I could just shout from the nearest roof

Jesus loves you

ego on the altar

like a holy bumble bee of accountability
humble me J.C.
right when the ugly head of my pride rears
all presumptuous and cocky
and while it's still ballooning
give it a good sting
send it whizzing around the room
deflating in an terrible hurry

oh, how stupid of me
as if I were on par with thee
as if I weren't the worst I know
and comparing myself with those who don't believe
I sound just like a Pharisee
as if I have already arrived
giving myself the highest grades
while I'm nowhere near sanctified

and what does it even mean?
to do this thing and say I don't care what they think
while I am to love them as I love myself
and how much do I care about my own thoughts?
a lot
but not enough
as in there lies the breeding ground for my every fault

oh, how I'd love to just cut me out
hand my everything over to God
let Him make the bad in me good
drain me of the dark and fill me with light

please God
without you, I rot
and if I take a single step askew
have mercy upon me and my blessed ability to walk
for I don't even deserve it
and if it's not about You
forgive me as I open my filthy mouth to talk
for I owe you my every word and breath
You gave me this tongue and these feet
You pulled me out of the desert
and You've protected me for so long
even when I was running in the other direction
ever since I was so young
oh how far I have come
and dare I take credit for any accomplishment
for You could end this at any second

and when You do and for now and forever

thank You, thank You, thank You God
You are everything
and only in You, am I found
only with You, am I something

the line drawn

there is nothing original
in doing what is wrong
and hoping that it will catch on
for that is exactly what the whole world has done

and again and again
only gets one numb
for forgetting that feeling of conviction
opens the door to all sorts of indulgence
let a little worldly dependency seep in
and before you know it
I'm a disciple with no discipline

but what's the harm?
after all, we're all sinners
and sinners sin
and rather than being joyful and thankful in all things
and continuously praying
it's so much easier to just cuss and complain
so easy to take a pill, swig or drag and just forget the pain
surely so

but to what am I called?
an ambassador I am
in a foreign land
representing the One

fully God
fully man
and everything I do should be in His name
for He is the One to thank
for everything

and I'm setting examples all the time
a role model to who knows?
well, He sure does
and with every faithful decision
as His will is done
His kingdom comes

but equally so
as nothing is neutral
and there's no such thing as being idle
for all things hinder that aren't beneficial
and any choice care of anything else only distances me from Him
I might as well spit in the face of my Lord and Savior
I might as well crucify Him again
every time I lose sight and seem to forget
giving in to this or that
whatever my gluttonous gut might want
taking part while knowing in my heart of hearts
this is not what life is about
and now it's about time I got back on track

ah, clarity
just as I crave and cringe
I release the desires from my death-grip
and they become His
praising and raising my arms with blooming fists
with some more of myself upon my palms
better off, I know, in His hands

and again I am freed
washed clean of fear and worry
He will satisfy my every need
and if it's meant to be
what I give up will be given back to me

God's best friend

we must walk for now
suffering long for the home we don't even know
while wearing only the leash we allow

and regardless of its style
we could be side by side our Master
or lazily falling behind and tugged along
choking ourselves as we charge ahead
or getting lost wearing none at all

in which case, He comes after us
leaving 99 behind if He must
and we might be happy for a while with whatever scraps
but hopefully before we're hit by a car
to Him we rush
once we've had enough
of the getting hurt while wandering off
and we learn that there's no real food to be found anywhere else

and once we know this much
we might okay some sort of harness
but when His and our plans don't match
it's hard not to presume what He wants for us
and so we sprint forward when He might intend a turn
and for a few steps, we might pull Him onward
but always, we just about hang ourselves before too long

and afterwards and almost surely, we do the opposite in reaction
wanting anything but to gag like that again
and/or just tired
we lag
and once in a while, a little bit is to be expected
but too much and we'll only be choked just the same and dragged
but for a stretch, He'd be happy to carry us instead
so long as we didn't flail and run away
tempted to return to our own vomit
starting all over again

but before it ever gets that bad, let's hope we learn
it's best to let Him set the pace
sure, sometimes it'll be time to run
but He'll always allow us a rest
and the least we could do is listen
when He prompts a change in direction

and once we really know the sound of His voice
and the trust is established
maybe we'd be okay without a leash
as long as we stay within a safe distance
really, still pretty much within arm's reach
but it's only this way that we are really free
not running astray
starving and left forever without Him
only next to Him can our walk go most favorably
all the way home

militianaries

when and where it's the norm
within the warmth of these walls and amongst ourselves
we speak of Him
our every reason
and as iron sharpens iron
like soldiers, we gather to sharpen our swords
but when we leave and where we live
do they know whose side we're on?
are we just ignoring the war?
we know it's raging on right now
in our members
outside that door
and all over
and as we might be busy looking in mirrors
running however many exercises
or doing whatever as if we haven't been given orders
the enemy takes ground
playing off of our fears
and our forgetfulness
somehow always remembering to convenience and comfort us

and it's not like we haven't heard it before
however seasoned or green that we are
if we know how to pronounce the Name and stand firm
we know enough to fight for the cause

the One worth living and dying for
the LORD

so let's unload and reload our mental munitions
knowing these verses are really the bullets
and our tongues, the guns
assembled in our mouths to shoot truths
and let's not think we can pick and choose who else to recruit
we ourselves were divinely drafted
and as more are miraculously added to His ranks
even when we're hated and laughed at
let us give thanks
as we fight for peace
and He puts us to use
serving the purpose
much greater than ourselves
oh what a relief it is
to know this isn't all about us

my God, we are so blessed
to even have this neighborhood barracks
our brothers across the globe are forced to meet in basements
and here we are in our state of the art training facility
but to them, the numbers are being added daily
what aren't we doing?

we know why we were born

thrown into this world
into this war
to make Him known
we know what we stand for
let us fear no man
and wherever we stand let's take ground for the LORD

Stage 2

THANKS FOR NOT STONING ME

b.c.

it's a boy!
white and ripe for a little middle-class suburbanite life
and already so well fed
he had to be c-sectioned into this ridiculously fortunate infancy
already blurring and turning innocently enough into a silly but chilly childhood
for as soon as one could
every breath was spent
looking forward to those wrapping-paper-ripping minutes
as to more, already hopelessly addicted
can a spoiled brat get a fix?
and having not yet graduated from single digits
already multi-faced
one of which, little neighborhood terrorist
yeah, just check out this little chunk of irony
this here was a bed-wetter bully
by day, tiny tyrant at recess
by night, piddling those pajama pants
poster-child for insecurity
and despite two married and loving parents
to suffer through tremendous privilege, he'd manage
all week, just dreading that one hour
as it was the worst of it
stand up, sit, kneel, stand, kneel, sit
we gotta say how many hails to Mary?
and hurry, better beat the traffic
just after yawning that same old song
always in the key of drone
and on his own
having asked for enough things
undelivered, or just too slow
he decided nothing was there
then of Cobain and Reznor, a devout follower
playing drums would become just one of some idol forms of worship
but playing hooky began to stick
by grade 6, so set on convincing and being convinced of any sickness
soon worried sick someone would not take his lying to himself
so serious

and though those eyes were soon cried dry
the crippling depression, he'd almost die trying to deny
and for about half a decade, it was like this
house and hell-bound
bored, in so many ways, blind
meanwhile, as uprooting twice left the fruit of any friendships behind
he was left enslaved to the mastering
living life through something else
games after comics
anything for a more effective hypnotist
or the next best mental escape hatch
always opting for the most graphic
and not above raiding the wallets of immediate family members
to feed these habits

oh, and to hate high school, never got nor took the chance
showing face for a week or two before slipping
into the predictable backslide
down down down into almost solidified thoughts of suicide
and just in time to empathize with the events at Columbine
but in this fashion, thank God, he'd do nothing more than fantasize
and about now, mom got a puppy
for the keeping her reclusive second son some sort of company
a cute and happy white highland terrier
terrified almost all day every day
next to him, nothing scarier
once routinely subjected
to our bi-polar basement boy's hellish self-pity
because hurting himself was only the beginning
by now, longing to feel something
cutting
this here was the bottom
from where, nowhere near looking up
or even out
no thanks help
but then came the life-saving stomachaches
could hardly eat a thing without having to soon crap out some brains
and with this, the madness was brought into focus
heck yes allergy test
and as the itching scratched all things tasty off the list
this taste of hell had for now, passed

and for now, he'd live
sort of

got a car, a job and senior year
but bring on the heart-breaking
all that porn ignited an already awkward virginity
burning a hole in his soul's pocket
labeled by him "lonely"
maybe music would attract that special someone
anyone
weird, sometimes funny guy
oh well, forever over the worst of it
or so he thought
college for whatever reason
various warehouse jobs
and while still a freshman, got really into drugs
pretty much anything short of meth, crack or heroin
so determined he was in his soul-searching and destroying
and it's a miracle he didn't land in prison
as sloppy as he was at dealing
briefly but long enough for a "give me everything you got man"
and somewhere in there
cleansed of the contracted gastrointestinal intolerances
and in light of this and despite his doubt
he gave thanks, to God
yeah, the One he didn't even believe in

and about now
learning a little something not-so-mainstream about 9/11
but reading a sort of self-help book for helping one's self to women
much like confidence in a can
now he was the one doing the heart-breaking
armed with poetry
the end of one two-year, mostly long-distance waste of innocence
marked the start of one all-too-common conquest
becoming one with one woman after another
number four
led to five
six
and all this despite the marijuana-induced performance issues
yeah, they don't tell you that smoking weed might lead to surgery
oh and how hesitant he was to believe
but twice
and yes, upon the parts of only a man's anatomy

un-phased
still living for the weekend
about as relaxing as a car accident
while still crashing forward with no direction
it'd be a while yet til mom's crash exposed much of himself to him
most concerned, consumed with sleeping around
so sayeth the doctors, "unable to have kids"
led to a miscarriage and a live-in girlfriend
mom's got Lou Gehrig's
and college coming to an end
Obama, what just happened?
where's that "hope" and "change"?
who are those men behind the curtain?
millions are starving, the world's ending
working away, who gives a flip about anyone's freaking lawn!?
and now imprisoned to the escaping
as she was seemingly the most effective means
and once again, not above selling weed
this time, to make ends meet
but growing more passionate for that towering mountain of
conspiracies
what is there to do?
protest?
stockpile guns? food?
or play videogames, get drunk, have sex and pretend
to not have a clue?
then, at last
even with all hope pretty much lost
cocky at class
who's this goofy-lookin' dude?
sporting a cross on top of an American flag?
well, our drug-dealing prince charming had just a few words
to say about that

"hey buddy, that's offensive"
"really? does it offend you that Jesus died for your sins?"
"uhh"
and from there
simple invitations had our guy finding himself high at a bible study
but paying pretty close attention, regardless
as what was once so far-fetched began making sense

in the Word
he saw himself
along with the true ways of this world
all in ways he had never before heard
and already current events were sounding pretty parallel
in the biblical department
noting the worldwide apostasy
the impending mark of the beast and one-world government
meanwhile, in the very book of the same name of a band
for which he once played bass
all coincidences, perhaps
"hey guys, so, what's this about offering our bodies
as a living sacrifice?"

hahaha
for once, beyond his own understanding, he'd just begin to look past
heck yes, Morpheus
hand over that red pill
the truth, and nothing less
though not yet knowing what to make of this Jesus
about now pro-Christian as anti, the elitists
and just a matter of weeks
on his own, weighing the evidence
once so resistant to the path, now of least resistance
the idea pops into his head to simply say the Name and mean it
Jesus, Jesus, Jesus
not long 'til he'd acknowledge his need for forgiveness and seek it
then, on an otherwise mundane Monday
they met
an hour passes and his God-send of a friend asks, "have you accepted Christ?"
his response?
"yes."
and in that moment
just as he was found in the finding of all he ever wanted
it's the strangest thing
he was crucified on the spot
yeah, he died
he died, and I was born
to live as designed
forevermore
for the Lord

gratitude for the taken for granted

if I just stop and think
I melt as I thank
forgiven as I am and for the giving of all that I take
right down to the gift of this next breath
not earned or owed to me
for all I deserve is death
such are the wages of anything not coming from faith
and this wincing is for this truth and its weight
for I can't even count how many times I fell astray today
but I sigh
knowing I'm okay
for on my own personal judgment day
there's someone else who will stand in my place
the perfect one whose paid my soul's price
Yeah, I'm saved
And with that, it seems
my best day on this earth is saved too
But for last
and until that glorious day I see Him face to face
I'll gratefully inhale His endless mercy and grace
exhale my passing away envy and hate

but again, let me stop and think
just as I find myself with a mind to speak
wait
I thank God for the ability to simply communicate
and as the words escape
from my heart remade
for now allowed to keep a beat
it keeps time to the song I pray my life sings
nothing but worship and praise
for Him
He who keeps my every atom from exploding and flying away
for why they don't, no one can hardly explain

and here, I'll consciously breathe again
pondering His mysteries
I contemplate how all this began
with His breath
speaking everything into being
breathing life into man
Or maybe, we should give credit to some big bang
as if the whole universe won some sort of cosmic lottery
yeah, I guess we're just supposed to feel lucky
to think time plus chance equals all of this
sad
this excuse to not give thanks
and pushed as fact
oh but, thanks be to you God, that anything and everything exists

breathe
and back I think
my God I was so blind
and now I see
thank you Lord for sight
but when these wild eyes cause me to stumble
sometimes I could just gouge them out
they are Yours to take away
and the same goes for these ears
despite all of that audible poison
my God, what a blessing it is to simply hear
and listen

He's never let me go hungry
I've always had a bed upon which to lay
and for my feet, a pair of shoes
my ability to walk, that's all Him too
but as for my direction
that's for me to choose
and that's for me to mess up
if I ever leave Him out
but He always brings me right back
to life
while letting me take that next breath
and for this one
I can't think of a better use
oh thanks be to God
for you

crosscheck

soon outlawed
saying anything of this sort out loud
just see how taboo it is now
and I'll only speak louder when no longer allowed

there is a God
and He loves us all so much
and because we're more in love with ourselves
our conscience just wasn't enough
to get us in
to let us in on who He really is
and so He sent to us His perfect Son
Jesus
died for us
rose again

how does that sound?
familiar, like a broken record?
or still the best news we've ever heard?
have we been bored all these years?
not sure why we attend this church like a chore
or does this most glorious truth still bring us to tears?
does His name cause us to turn and cringe?
or grin and change?

the turning

uh oh
the Christian's got the microphone
and by "Christian", you know
I really mean "hypocritical, judgmental homophobe"
what could he possibly have to say that I don't already know?
is he going to tell me I'm going to hell
just 'cause I don't fit some mold?
please
and don't even get me started on that big book of old
no, I haven't read the thing, surely full of holes
just a long and ugly game of telephone
how many translations and through how many hands?
and just how faulty is man?
what a joke
who even cares what happened 2000 or so years ago?
I can hardly wait for the day science explains it all away

ah, but here he goes
shoving his religion down my throat as if he knows
why doesn't he leave well enough alone?
I'm a good person
and if there's a heaven
I'm sure God or whatever will let me in
it's not like I've ever killed anyone

so who does this guy think he is?
trying to tell me what I need
sorry buddy if you're so weak
that you have to cling to some outdated belief
whatever works for you, just don't push it on me
your routine
your crutch
you read your book
meet every week in that country club of a church
sing your songs, pray your prayers
and somehow, that's enough?

please
you're kidding only yourself
you're as lost as the rest of us
no one can know what's really true
and that's the alpha and omega of the truth
if it weren't, then let's see some proof
and I ain't talking about a supposed face on a chunk of toast
nor some random and dirty piece of cloth
and not a couple steel beams found at ground zero
in the shape of a cross
miraculous healings?
yeah right, why didn't they make the news?
believers dying in rejoice?
that's just nuts
but regardless, if He is risen, let's see some wounds
Yeah, let's see the big man coming in the clouds
let's see Him strike me down
oh, you're telling me I gotta believe first before I see some signs
and it all makes sense?
but of course
and perhaps then I could be just as closed-minded

but just how open-minded am I?
if I'm not even willing to give Him a try
and if He claims to be the only way
I guess I better make damn sure He's just a lie

so, who is this Christ?
crucified
and for me?
but why?
and what of all the wars fought in His name?
the Crusades?
here I thought Jesus was all about peace
either someone's got it wrong
or they're just looking to pass off the blame
for didn't He say to love your enemy?
and isn't "thou shalt not kill" somewhere in there?
and speaking of those rules
it's kinda funny
that the ten commandments were removed from schools
and come to think of it
Christians on TV are portrayed as nothing but fools
what's up with that?
if we're supposed to be some sort of Christian nation
and no one seems too concerned
about the Bible being illegal in some 53 countries and counting
something tells me these "Christian" politicians wouldn't know
the first thing about following the Son of Man
oh my God, are you thinking what I'm thinking?
Holy strategical misrepresentation bat-man
we've been had
and how hateful I've been
when to me, of Christianity, my every negative thought was given
don't you see?
every time He's been claimed only for some selfish gain
that's man, not Him

so, where's the hope?
what of all the things I know I shouldn't do but can't seem to help?
this whole world is at the end of its rope
and I can't do anything about it
by myself

God?

well, who do you say that I am?
come to me
follow me
and for you, I have a plan

nearing the ending

any day now
out of the clouds
upon a white horse
and with a sword from His mouth
God's gonna clean house
and as the friends of this world are busy
pooping their pagan underpants
I'll be singing the praises
and even if this shell is killed in the process
cause I know my God's got this
and He delivers on His promises
all for His good pleasure
and knowing home is where the heart is
Heaven's where I keep my treasure
and pre or post trib
I ain't banking on being raptured
at least not before I get the chance to really suffer
you know, some disgrace for The Name
in of which, many have and will come
you know, false teachers leading the droves astray
but fretting, I ain't
cause firm in my faith is where I intend to stay
even if I am the subject of every man's hate
'til the end
whence I am saved
from that unfortunately literal place
of many names
you may know it as the lake of flames
but no matter how many books Rob Bell sells, hell won't be erased
it's kinda too bad every stinking one of us deserves God's worst
and until you understand this
you can't comprehend let alone accept God's amazing grace
oh, how sweet the sound
Almost makes me look forward to that awful day of judgment
counting down

but a few things must happen yet
as written
some good old fashioned plagues and famine
wars and rumors of wars
and two thirds or more destroyed for lack of knowledge
yes, off, most will be polished

but still, you might ask
how can a good god exist?
as all the evil in this fallen world persists
but you really oughta give that question a little twist
considering the evil things you yourself think
perhaps by now
there's some tortures upon myself you'd like to inflict
or that feeling you're feeling just might be the Holy Spirit
sent to comfort, sent to convict

but never mind this
comforted as we are, unto boredom
in America, so God blessed
and with most image bearers still walking dead in those transgressions
this might yet be a zombie apocalypse

and trust me, soon, nothing else will make any sense
as we're ushered into cashless-ness
and when it all hits
you won't catch me praying to no puppet president
nor paying any respects to big-business politics
unlike the desperate masses

Oh welfare, wal-mart government save us!
that's just what we plan to do, yes
and with some useful work, a place to rest and microchips
you'll be blessed
sure, we'll let you exist
just deny Jesus
by now we know His followers are all intolerant terrorists
just look at all the wars religion's caused

so they'll say
their kind being the kind waging them all
in His name

oh well, at least I've found peace
knowing that the powers of this dark world will meet
nothing but defeat
but still, you may know not of what I speak

now if only I could make those wooden eyes see
and if only I could awaken a soul
but all I can do is plant and water a seed
He's the One that makes it grow
God, please
some good soil

and seeing as they did much to awaken mine
I still can't help but tell the devil's secrets
why?
just so I can some day say I told you so?
no, brother
just so on that day it all goes down
down is how your spiritual pants might not get caught
when all of this is lost
no ifs about it
start letting go now

and do not fear for that already rotting body
just know the source of my sense of urgency
for the state of things is far from peachy
because His perfect and well-deserved judgment is coming
and only does He tarry, for He is rich in mercy
and the time or day, no one knows
it's just time to pray that we wake up before He shows up
and shows us
just how worthy He is
and reacquainting us all with number one and two
of the ten commandments
He'll think a thought and erase all graven images
on every golden calf, He'll make like Moses
His awesome wrath, He'll no longer hold back
sovereignty separating the wheat from the chaff
casting the latter half to weep and to where teeth gnash

so, dear brothers
be not deceived
and others
expect to parish
or repent and believe

long lost

it's been a minute
what, maybe a year now?
I see your status update
you see mine
no comment

why?
once so close, so cool, so kind
now far apart, in the dark, blind
no doubt these and similar thoughts also cross your mind
but again, why?

did you change?

no

it was I

and with no reason or explanation
enough for you
to be changed too
you'd catch me quoting of all things, the Book
until then, the butt of so many a joke
unread experts we once were
thinking we knew what it implied
and now I doubt you could even believe those eyes
and writing this off as a phase
you might've tried
as I'm sure, like me, you didn't expect we would end up on opposing sides
but soon, my every word, you couldn't help but hate
and you might've even felt kinda betrayed
as I'd claim to be "saved" while giving thanks and praise
standing for none other than the worthy One we were once so united in standing against
so set in our ways
back then, making a total mockery of Who who is now, my identity

how could this have happened?
did I go crazy?
nay, my dear friend
or maybe
crazy in love
'til the end
forsaking all else
all this stuff
because, next to perfect, everything kinda sucks
and when I gave good a good look
absolute infatuation met abject disgust
for myself

and on that note
sorry if I've ever treated you like a project
I've come to know the best thing ever and I just want to share it
I'd convince, argue, or shake this into you if I could
really, for you to know Him too, I'm quite desperate
because already, I miss you
and there is such a thing as too late

better than bacteria

today, we have reason to celebrate
yeah, however many years ago
on this day
you joined us
I and others might say
in including you
God chose to bless you and us

as unique as you are
you fill a roll and you have a place
you're a part of His body
His story and His fame is your life's purpose
as unique as you are

but, thinking about it, this date really only marks your entrance
there are plenty others at least just as significant
I mean, it was about 9 months before then
when your mom and your dad, well, you know...
and so, fearfully and wonderfully inside of your mother
He'd begin the meticulous knitting together
and yet, way before that is when God thought you up
along with the good works in which you would walk
before the earth's foundations were laid, in fact
and really that's how and when we all got started

or is it?
or are we all here because the universe farted?
for lack of a better term
yeah, you know, perhaps something came from nothing
and an inexplicable lightning bolt sparked it
and from that, you get the sun, moon and stars
add some trillions of years, and well, here we are
just mathematical miracles
pointless vessels of genetic material
no better than bacteria

but really now
let's get empirical
let's look at the science
gosh darn it
stupid thermodynamics
even after all that we've progressed
I guess "survival of the fittest" has its limits
seeing as how we must've just somehow missed the big one
yeah someday, we'll all be dead
and I guess that's just how it is

oh well, if only they could see us now
I bet our ancestral amoebas would be pretty proud
having taken that brave leap of faith
from one unexplainable cell to every living thing ever
or maybe they'd be kinda jealous and sad
them and all those missing links nowhere to be found
conveniently left behind
right along with simple cell-division
phased out in favor of sexual reproduction
but what, wait, okay, Mr. brilliant biologist sir
please just honestly riddle me this
exactly how, when or why did that happen?
you know, the opting for getting one cell from two
rather than two cells from one
two genders where there was once supposedly none?
and since when are mutations so beneficial?
again, thanks be to evolution
that hit or miss somehow managed to sell sex cells into the mix
oh, how thoughtful of luck to let us fit together
like so many pleasurable puzzle pieces
and humans, determine your own context
just please don't go involving any kids

ah, but who am I to pass judgment?
as I was taught in schools public
like you, I'm on par with any bug or insect
just a freak of nature, cosmic accident
fortunate enough
to be however many steps ahead of our simian friends
surely anticipating the typing of Hamlet
oh, and I can just see it now
our great-great-great grand-monkey-parents
just waiting to waste their random chance lives
being hypnotized by the latest gadgets
but seriously now, we better get off our butts
before we know it, those apes will be catching up
just give it enough time
soon they'll too be reading, writing and speaking in rhyme
yeah, and they'll set up courts and judges
and declare throwing their own crap to be a crime
just wait and see
some chimpanzees are already using sign-language
before you know it, they'll graduate from that cage and rightfully
move right on to college

yeah
call me skeptic
but when I look in pretty much any direction
I don't see a whole lotta chaos
I see beauty, potential and purpose
intentionality and intelligence
I'd say I'm blessed
perhaps I'm biased
but we all have the same evidence
and I'm no expert
but it seems to me
the only scientists given any credence these days are atheists
bent on convincing us that everything created itself, nothing matters
and we're all worthless
such is the worth of all the doubt in the world
so why in the world is it a surprise?
suicide being on the rise
amongst a population dehumanized
force fed a curriculum of fairy tales and flat-out lies
led to believe wholeheartedly in nothing
taught to take and defend only the most un-offensive position
all the while, systematically addicted to distraction
millionaire barbarians? Kardashians? what's your poison?
or are you feeling a little tired? under the weather? low self-esteem?
oh, just buy that thing, take this pill and keep watching your TV
yeah, go to school, get a job and start a family
just so your kids can do the exact same thing
don't you see?
you don't see any meaning
because there isn't any
outside of Jesus Christ
disagree?
the Lord is Lord over all
slave or free
so remember this
when you too bow
as written, every knee

and if biology is the study of life
y'all oughta study Christ
cause He's it
and the Truth
so science, please continue your pursuit
I only pray it's not in vain and you too find, in time
that He is the Way
and if you happen to be on a quest for knowledge,
you just might wanna love correction
cause there's no denying
something's wrong with us humans
some might say we ain't done evolving
pretty sure we're just fallen
and some of y'all need to read up on your Genesis
cause, whatever the context, whether cult or science class
this line about humanity's potential to progress to a god-like status
kinda eerie how much that sounds like what the serpent told Eve
yeah, 'ye shall be as gods'

please, spare me the deception
get behind me Satan
I see right through your unoriginal sin
in six days, as written, God created this creation
not a bunch of aliens
messing with the junk of whoever they abduct
behaving just like demons
yeah, pretty scary stuff
but with my little bit of faith
I'll continue to celebrate
today and everyday
knowing you and I are no mistake

consider the birds
are you not much more valuable than they?
it's in God's image that you were made
precious enough that He would die to save
and I pray you call His name

be blessed

happy birthday

everyday backwards ballet

so wildly under control
we are the foolish things of His choosing
just tools for the King's using
and knowing there's no higher calling
only in this and in our weaknesses, we take pride
once lost, now found to confound the wise
those who so strive to feel alive
realize
to really live
first, you must die

yes, if it is the narrow road leading to life that you intend to find
it is the self that must be denied
otherwise, don't say you weren't warned as you free-fall
through that deadly gate, so wide

now, thinking back
I sure don't remember getting a chance to decide
when, where, who or especially, why
because, like you, I'm here on borrowed time
this is to say, you are not yours
as I am not mine
and however strange this might sound
know, only in total submission is true freedom found
and what this world of a stage calls free
is really the worst sort of slavery
and us?
yeah, even in shackles
and next to those seemingly getting away with murder
we are infinitely more free
crazy, I know

and for now
sorry
but some of your favorite things are likely the heaviest of chains
maybe that flashy gadget from which you can't seem to look up
surely that shameful habit you can't put down or give up
yeah, that urge is a curse of a thirst
for which, there is a cure that will purge even the worst
and sure, we're slaves too
but what masters us is exactly what frees
for we know, we were made and freed to perform

and although our style might at times look somewhat interpretive
anyone may join the narrative
no auditions

just know in your broken bones that you are His

consider this your official invitation
and although it costs everything
admission is really free
because He has long ago paid for you and me

you know they expected a conquering king
and got a loon nailed to a tree
but wouldn't you know it, He rose after day three
forever taking His rightful place in all of history
for over Him, even death has no mastery

and through His merciful breaking of our legs
we progress
and we dance
sure, at times, we might look like a mess
like everyone else
but we mess-ups confess

and though we might stumble
as He directs our steps
He never lets us fall
and though we must improvise at all times
no true devotees go solo with this free-style
nor start another production
for at the end of the day
we know there's really only one show in town

and until He Himself appears for that finale
we'll heed His cues
and we'll take our places as the opposed proponents to those
those upon whose heads our good deeds heap hot coals
we are but poor, weak fools
rejoicing as we mourn those
clinging to the everything they have to lose
so in love with this age about to exit stage right
we can't help but pity the prosperous
and the strong, we lead
for we know
He is the why
for He is the cause
this is His story
His production
and only He deserves applause

God's hats

unto us
lowly humans
us men, women and children
from every time, tribe, tongue and nation
yes, unto us
One was given
One worth celebrating
worth our everything

You
from before "in the beginning"
and beyond "it is finished"
You who were, are and always will be holy, holy, holy
to think, You came to us

and who are we?
that You should care?
and so much?
making Yourself as helpless babe
and taking all of the blame
all of humanity's filthiness placed upon Your shoulders
right where all of the world's governments will someday rest

but until then
what sense am I to make of this stress?
growing old
losing touch
gripped by debt with hills of bills to pay
immediate and extended family tensions
forever failing relationships
all work and no play
health issues
politics
car trouble
boredom
loneliness

but to all of this, what do You say?

cast those cares
this is all part of the process
brace yourself like a man
and know, the wise heed advice
yes
and next to Yours
any other so-called wisdom is but utter foolishness
and of which, whoever lacks
need only ask
and in of which, infinite
only You could think just how to twist
the ugliest and worst of things
the most evil of schemes
into the most beautiful and glorious
surely You know our struggles and stress
having felt it all, yes

and who again is wise?
but You who created all of this
from the vastness of the cosmos to the smallest of particles
all unfathomably complex
and so thoughtfully placed
from earth's and everything's position in space
to ours within our families, jobs and various spheres of influence
and by You, all simply spoken into existence
and by Your will, holding together
even the nails that held you there
and to think
with a thought or a wink, it could have all been over

but no

because again, You care
while we were yet enemies
and much like a Father, raising us up
oh, how delighted You are as we learn to walk
and while we're yet young, so loud and clear is Your voice
but as we grow and as You know, once in awhile
we just might be given a choice
and whatever we decide, to You, it's no surprise
even if we'd run and hide
almost starve and die before coming to ourself
even as Your slave, we'd be better off
but we return to You running to us
and us, You make Your children
for whom the fattened calf, You would slay
clothe us in Your righteousness and celebrate

and if children, then heirs
of an unthinkable inheritance
provided we share
in Your sufferings
and speaking of which
surely You're troubled by what troubles us
but someday
soon enough
You'll make peace
and starting now with our feet
fitted with these shoes and made things of beauty
equipped with the news and the Name to carry
for just a few steps away from comfort, enormous is the need
but endless is Your peace
of which, You are the Prince
even amidst tremendous tragedy

yes, unto us
a Son is given
making You and us family

the great play

under the lights like a microscope
where one acts, portrays or depicts
or where ever the prying eyes of an audience are glued upon us
we are our own worst critics

trust me

yeah, here is where we really examine ourselves
and it's the end of the world
when I'm the one forgetting lines
taking a wrong step
missing cues
messing up

and a lot begins as just a little bit
the trick is getting back on track and quick
and my missing marks starts a trend
but here it is oh so easy to consider this plank
next to your speck
doing the exact same things
because you see, I'm the lead
and you're support
but I suppose, from your point of view, the opposite is true
and as you might stumble, fumble and draw a blank
silently, violently, you pray
while I know they don't notice and it'll be okay
with the next cue, you'll know what to do and say

but take this line of thought off stage
and just how many roles do we have?
you know, we know we ought behave
as in the light of the day
at all times, otherwise, aren't we genuinely fake?
yeah, of what are we most passionate?
are we perhaps ashamed to say?
yeah, pretty sure we really are who we are in private

so, how is anyone not an actor, or hypocrite?

know
even when you're alone
you're in the spotlight
and like you, I have no excuse
even on opening night
for the Director so clearly directed
that it's only for my faults that I can take credit
because He knows and He showed us what would be perfect
having written the script
and having come down and acted this out Himself
in full dress

and so, to do our best
even when we're by ourselves
we practice
and even before a most critical audience
it's only Him we ought aim to impress

for even when we were amongst the most heinous of hecklers
He is the one who cast us

and we know, our acting could never be good enough
but when the show is over
all of our mistakes, He forgets
and His perfect performance in us is all that's left
again, so long as we're on the cast

and with that
as He said
it is finished

sentenced to freedom

check it out
I'm free
I do what I want
as I please
yeah, this world is my oyster
whatever that means
and "do what thou wilt" actually sounds pretty good to me
for as fate would have it
what I really want is only right
and I've pretty much forgotten what boredom feels like
ever since by grace through faith got my priorities straight

in an instant
I went
from hating the things I now love
and from loving the things I now hate
oh, to those things I'm now ashamed of
I was a slave
and oh snap
yeah, like that
I was changed

it was getting dark
sitting in my car
parked
with one sentence
and one witness
this war, this Spirit, this fire was sparked
believing in my heart what my mouth would then confess
and my coming so far would start

thanks be to God
He meets us where we're at
sets free to be who He meant
and to this day
I know in my bones
the Greatest Commandment
and set free to act it out
or at least try
with all of my heart
soul and mind
so don't mind me
as I thank Him again for being strong where and when I am weak
and here I'll take a walk, run, hop, skip and leap
in that very faith
which might have once only sounded to me
like a fairy tale's excuse
for a big ugly list of don'ts and do's
but Jesus ain't a set of rules
He's not just a good guy
and He's no joke
and as all who seek Him, find Him
He's not wishing that any should perish

but this freeing faith
I or no one could do a thing to obtain
or maintain
for if we could, it wouldn't be grace

yes, and plucked as we were out of this world
to be not of this world
I'm convinced
nothing can pluck us from His grasp
with the breadth, width, height and depth
of this universe times itself
yeah, think all of time, space and mass
squared
and on our side
almost doesn't seem fair
and seeing as He's already won, we're free now even to fail

wait
what was I saying?
give me a second
oh, this is embarrassing

not really
cause the worst of me has already been broadcast
from that cross
yeah, at Calvary
considering my countless criminal acts and thoughts
that should've been me
a quarter century wasted worshipping self and anything else
and not to mention all my sins since

and besides, it's not me nor my name you need to remember
I'm just a messenger
really, a walking, talking reminder
made and remade to bring Him attention and enjoy Him forever
and again, nothing I've ever done made me deserving of this
in fact, quite the opposite
like the next
yeah, we're not much
really, just dust
and yet, more than conquerors
simply unable to make Him love us
any more or less

so brothers, go ahead as you're led
eat, fast, circumcise, baptize
speak in tongues and have your fun
just know, none of this saves or sanctifies
these are only outward signs
just check Romans 14 and particularly the last line
and while you're at it, check again Ephesians 2: 8 and 9
belief is the free gift of God
move on to verse 10 and you'll see
we're really only freed to respond

yeah, we're His hands and feet
and I don't know about you
but since I've been bought by the blood
to thank Him, I simply cannot do enough

and thankful now for how free we are
until we miss and reminisce about just how free we were
I pray we don't wait until it's illegal
before we treat the Word and His commission like it is
vital

my God, I pray someday soon we'll see revival
before denying You is a matter of survival
but I suspect that's just what it might take
to make us seize the day
everyday an adventure
oh, for Your sake
wake us up so we might live it up
free from the sting of death, the ways of this world
and this stinkin' flesh
free and ready to meet You who we confess
yes
make us bold before those who can kill the body
and after that
nothing else
yeah, we're free to go out like William Braveheart Wallace
they'll never take our freedom
for it's where the Spirit of the Lord is

and it's for freedom that we are freed
yes, He set us free
and we are free indeed

the fearful wonderful

if only I could speak
I would talk you out of the unspeakable
or maybe I'd say I'm sorry
for my apparently terrible timing
though, you know, it wasn't up to me
and if I wasn't so innocent
yeah, I just might plead guilty
to whatever earned me a sentence of death
but you as my witness
I haven't done anything yet
haven't even taken my first breath
but perhaps doing your best
to avoid a trial
it seems, my deadly crime is my being inconvenient
yeah, my crime is being

so, here I am
maybe getting in the way of your plans
and just wanting a chance
here, where my life isn't my right
it's your choice
of which, you can wash your hands
in this fatally free country
for a couple hundred bucks
so dead set it seems
on separating church and state
but what has that to do with us?

and in this womb with no view
maybe I'm just a deadbeat tenant
taking residence inside of you
and making you a little fat
as if it weren't cute
but unable to pay rent of any sort
I can only pray you don't kick me out
oh, my gracious landlord

but if you do
or if you ever have
there's grace for even that
oh, of all the siblings I never had
not allowed to live as they weren't
yeah, even the spilling of unborn blood
and the resulting guilt
yeah, it'll take just a little more blood to cover it
nothing short of perfect
and long ago spilled
after a conception, pregnancy and birth
came a life lived, equally immaculate
and coming close to His holiness
no one will, does or did
for even when they thought He was dead
they looked again and found Him risen
just as He said
accept this and you'll find yourself forgiven
even of the worst of things
even abortion

but, please
if only I could speak
mommy
daddy
I'd say please
let's be family

I don't care how I got here
mommy, if you were raped, I'm so sorry
and daddy, if you didn't mean to father me
it's too late, but it'll be okay
I don't care how much or little we have
I just, want to live
with you

or I'm sure there's someone
someone who maybe can't have a baby
more able
who'd love to love me

oh, if only I could speak
maybe I'd scream
for after just six weeks
this heart beats
and for sure, two weeks later
if not already
this brain thinks
about what, who knows?
maybe I dream
of you, us
the future
and all that could be

a picture of forever

see what a profound mystery
this 'big day' makes
and perhaps a reproduction
someday
but for now, the beginning of a mural
this doodle or snapshot, if you will
mutually captured by these sort of modelers
in not a thousand words
but two

"I do"

and with this choice voiced
this husband and wife
hold fast
for life
and to what might feel like a moment for a Kodak

and in the midst of the flash
the vapor that is this life
oh, though this bliss is so blessed
it's hardly to be missed in the life next

as for now, simply serving its purpose
with roles equally different
let him serve and her submit
and with the washing of the water of the Word
like Photoshop
this picture is made perfect
in love
they walk
the rest of the Way
together, as they illustrate
yes, from here on out
another perspective they'll give and take
as He'll paint and they portray
the Way

of Christ and the Church, I speak
and like His pursuit
of us
as they or the like, seek
this is the fruit
of the Kingdom and His righteousness

but if God's not God
do vows mean a thing?
does anything?

and in holy matrimony
as it was meant to be
like all else, this points to Him
the Bridegroom and His Bride
the picture He has always had in mind
when it was and it will be good again
the fall resolved by the resolution
the highest of highs

and despite the ups and downs in between
this image, these graphics
so intelligently designed
with each brush stroke so abstractly concrete
so messily positioned are the pixels
in health and in sickness unto sleep
let no man separate what He has brought together
yes, because this is, it was meant to be
a picture of forever

Stage 3

EVEN IN WAR
I AM AT PEACE

pickup lines

when we were just kids
oh, how intense was that first kiss?
we nearly flipped our lids
when barely even pressing together our lips

and at first, I froze
but as terrified as I was
I figured this is what a guy does
and so, shaking in my shoes
covered with the bumps of a goose
leaning in, I snuck a smooch

and in a daze for days

but as the years elapsed
and our flesh got its way
this so-called romance and maybe many came and collapsed
unable it would seem, to agree on a pace
almost always too much too fast
and our good thing turned bad and was gone in a flash
leaving us moving on and on to someone else
and with whatever other pretty face
we couldn't wait to say goodbye to some more innocence
couldn't wait to cross the line of whatever's next
until, before we knew it, we were bored with sex

irony
how now, we'd be led to believe
and by nothing but those misleading feelings
or lack thereof
yeah, whatever this was, we knew even then
it wasn't real love
yeah, whatever following our hearts led us into
following our hearts now, we see
as good as it might've once felt
any or all of that wasn't 'meant to be'

fast forward
rinse and repeat and repeat

and soon enough, thank God
the heaviness of our hearts would bring us to our knees
where we were, are and will be
cleaned, redeemed and made complete
yes, it was for us, former enemies, that God had to bleed
and instantly satisfied was and is the long-running longing
for some one
by simply acknowledging our need
for Him
the One who never rejects
never lets down, really forgives and forgets
yeah you know all of that so-called love we've let go to waste
all of those unspeakable mistakes
as far as He's concerned, erased
and that love for which we've been looking
in every wrong place
you and I have been granted access
to the love greatest
for there is no greater love than this
one laying His life down for His friends
as that's just what He did

and you know, I could say we found Him
by His grace
but I really should say He found us
for we were the ones who were surely lost
and however messed up we are
it's only broken hearts that He wants
and not to be tied up in a routine or religion
just knowing that the great divide has been crossed
and we're healed and freed by the divine friendship that results
and you better believe it
this Friend comes with benefits
namely His Spirit
oh, so sweetly He comforts and convicts
yes, in us, He took up residence
and we haven't been the same since

and knowing that upon Him, we can cast that broken past
yes, upon Him, we can unload our massive baggage
and should He have someone for us
someone suitable for marriage
it is only God's love for us that his and her
yours and my love should image
and it's no wonder that He uses so much family language
it's cause God wants a relationship
and the picture a husband and wife paints
it's to Christ and the Church that this connection points
and consummation provides only a glimpse
oh, for how great His love is for us
it will take Him an eternity to pour out
if we only love Him most
yes, death itself will not do us part
but mark the start
for He is the Bridegroom
and we are the Bride
and with Him, we get an eternal honeymoon

but in the meantime
as convinced as I am that He is
and knowing there's no greater blessing than this
I guess that would make you
of all that's ever happened to me
second best
so, I must ask
with me, will you do this thing?
right, for life and for His glory
yes, let's paint that picture

will you marry me?

the linchpin

I got nothing
no grasp on reality
no reason for living
no hope or peace
and certainly no certainty
yeah, no nothing

that is, if He isn't risen

yeah, if it simply ain't true
if He's still in that tomb
God might as well have never even walked this earth as a dude
and my whole worldview falls through

for real
generations come and go
the earth remains
toiling under the sun
what does man gain?
by the sweat of one's brow until returning to the ground
ALL is vain
and not just every gathering
gathering in His name

whose Name, I don't even have to say
as no other faith
no other way can deliver what He claimed
nor do they aim

loving the dark
agnostic or not
those who don't want to know God won't
while they must admit, nothing is what they've got
just a great big, "I don't know"
and neither do I
again, if He didn't rise

and I'm not talking resuscitation
like what happened to good ol' Lazzy
for he eventually died again
but no, just as He showed the two on that road to Emmaus
a doubtful Tommy
and every eye-witness
Jesus was first to show us what friends of His get
a new, as-it-was-meant-to-be body
now, that's what I call 'cross-fit'
yes, the resurrection is just about everything
for without it, no one's forgiven
we're still in our sins
and no one's headed for heaven

yeah, fam
there's no over-emphasizing this doctrine
check verse 9 of Romans 10
just what is essential for salvation?
confess Him
and with one's heart, believe what?
oh, there it is
He is risen

or is He?
man, if He didn't rise
His every disciple has been living and dying for a lie
from the 12
quickly fear stricken with His being smitten, as written
but emboldened something bonkers
after seeing Him again
walking, talking, breaking bread
and so sure that they did, martyred
out of those 12, 10

but if you think He didn't rise
for your doubt, would you die?

and starting with the stoning of Stephen, Acts 7
to this day, the good news and its proof spread
like a life-changing, soul-saving pandemic
and despite all of that devil-driven division
while what makes a denomination Christian is that they agree
He is risen

oh, and yes He is
otherwise, those suffering for this belief
like those praising Him from prison
are again, doing so for nothing

and here, maybe forgetting to thank God
for the air-conditioning
we might have yet to be considered so worthy
as all will be persecuted that want to live a life, Godly
and if in Christ, our hope is for this life only
yeah, Osteen
we are most to be pitied
clinging to just another man-made religion
like so many mythologies
attempting to earn and suppose one's way to heaven
and like them
it's funny that this would be, silly superstition
hasn't come and gone with the changing of seasons
along with how ever many who have claimed to be as He
because Him, they could never copy
yeah, good luck mustering up a perfect sacrifice
one that would have to similarly have died for us
but for us, no other supposedly holy guy has died
let alone, after the fact, rise
that's cause our guy, yeah, our God is alive
and news of His being raised has stayed
as His Word has yet to pass away
for like Him, it seems, His Word too conquers the grave

but maybe, as far as you're concerned, we can't prove this scientifically
sorry, that's because this most-poignant event is a question of History
and only a matter of time before no matter of opinion
because, not only is Christ risen, but coming again

Son of Maggot

imagine maggots
teeming and twisting and feeding on some bloated carcass

and along comes you
in your infinite benevolence
in your unimaginable compassion
you take notice
and of all the ways to be or feel
you care
yeah, you see what they are
what they're doing and you could vomit
you're so grossed out
but still, you care
and you can't help it
in fact, you love each and every maggot
and so much, you hurt
wow, how weird are you?
how strangely awesome
that you'd not just walk away and forget them
or wash them away, but you promised, not again
but no, even in your repulsion, you care
even with your ways, so above theirs
while of you, they're largely if not totally unaware
though you might've been, actually all along
they don't even see that you're there

but a faithful few might believe
there's more
thinking rightly of themselves as a sort of lower life-form
and imagining something or someone
kind of like you
a power higher
but they can't hardly grasp the concept of a human
let alone, know the depths of your love for them

so, what can you do?
maybe provide some fresh meat
but do they show gratitude?
and just try washing their little maggot feet
well, isn't that cute?
show yourself in everything
in their every surrounding
they still haven't got a clue
sure, they might love whatever you provide
but not you
and even if you whisper
ever so soft
they don't understand
they can't
but with one or two
you might get through
deliver a message or commandment
but so soon, they forget
become a fly and fly away
only to crawl all over some excrement

what's the use?
but you don't and you can't give up
so wonderfully determined to have your way
as still, you love them so much
and love, it doesn't fail

oh, if only down you could stoop
and become one
speak the local maggot dialect
replace your clean clothes with some squirmy skin
you'd let them know where you came from
live a perfect maggot life
die the perfect maggot death
all for them

Son of Maggot
Son of Man

connecting dots

question
what in the world is going on?
yeah, who are we going to war with now?
what doesn't cause cancer?
and how many gazillions are we in debt?
I don't know, but pretty sure something's wrong
especially when most don't know, nor want to
yeah, nothing to see here folks
move along, move along

ok, whether we're in a room or not
here's the elephant
cliché, I know
but how about today, we talk about it?
don't worry, I won't ask you to think too hard
just consult your gut
for it knows, however willfully ignorant we are

yeah, left or right
black or white
rest in peace M.J.
pretty sure you were onto something
singing,
"all I want to say is that, they don't really care about us"

oh but, don't worry about it
just trust the government
and be happy you're alive
here and for now
in this nation
"the greatest"

yeah, one nation under surveillance
and you know, I don't even have to get into specifics
it's not like I could even scratch the surface
in these few minutes
but something tells me, it's all probably a lot worse
than even I think it is

oh but please, don't talk to me about politics
or religion

hmm, funny how THOSE topics are off limits
often ending a conversation if even mentioned

yeah, please, just do your duty as a citizen
vote
go to church or don't
whatever you do, just keep to yourself, your opinion
and don't get too impassioned
they're listening
and while you're at it, don't pay so much attention
because it's upsetting
that feeling of going in the wrong direction
helplessly
hopelessly

curious
just how did the holocaust happen?
did they see it coming?
and are we any less naive?
remember, history forgotten will repeat
and writing and rewriting it
yeah, so who's REALLY steering the ship?
could it be the filthy, stinkin' rich?
yeah, and what is it that makes them tick?
who's best interests do they have in mind do ya think?
and when any one of us useless eaters kicks the bucket
do they even give a flip?
and will most of us know better?
I wonder
than to take the chip
and how about this?
what do you suppose they worship?
yeah, who's their guiding voice of choice?
when they say it's a tragedy
to let a catastrophe go to waste

at least Adolf had the guts to be the brains and the face
for it seems now that the tyrants of ever since
have only sought to learn from his mistakes

but really now
can you name the last political figure that delivered?
like, maybe a fraction of what was promised

we know, it's all rhetoric to get into office
and from Eden to Washington
curious that anyone would be so anxious
to have the devil himself work them like a ventriloquist
and you know the greatest trick the devil ever pulled
was convincing the world he didn't exist
but take one look at this world and it's flippin' obvious
with 20,000 dying daily of starvation
and 30 million slaves currently in circulation
but if we're all just pond scum and stardust
yes sir, Mr. Anarchist Atheist Secular Humanist
why or how would or could you ever be pissed?
every injustice can be justified as "survival of the fittest"

yeah, Satan, that prince of the power of the air
the god of this world
is behind all of this
and that's god with a little "g"
and c'mon guys, with all of the earth's kingdoms
is it a surprise that a government who lies would be on his side?
blinding the minds of those who just can't seem to believe
and brothers, is it any wonder?
I mean, against who or what is it that we struggle?
but whoever you are
take heart
for these deceiving Caesars just might be the most deceived
because it's with Almighty God whom they compete
and there's no defeating Him
yeah, those playing God have God as their competition
evidenced by the everything they've got their crooked hands in
everything they glorify
from the garbage on television to the dumbed-down education system
all things politically correct, main-stream or otherwise
pretty much nothing but anti-Christian
no sedated adult or impressionable child left behind
when it comes time to evolve or die

and sure
some rulers, authorities and principalities may claim Him
but please, by its fruit, you'll know a tree
and like you, I just might like to think
that these are some well-dressed sheep
but who are we kidding if we say
that they're not wolves who masquerade

for if they really were God's peeps
pretty sure they'd be all about His ways
you know unbalanced scales, He hates
yeah, and they'd implement some real change
and in which case, just maybe JFK'd

and aside from the Messiah
don't fall for any notion of peace
cause it's false and temporary
labeled "tolerance"
man-made or perhaps care of some supposed E.T's
all the while fulfilling all sorts of prophecies
they'll establish their pseudo utopia
doing everything they can in the meantime
to make some Stalin-esque communism sound like a good idea

and just waiting for the day
freedom from religion lands us Christians in prison
or separation of church and state crucifies us
outside the city gates
like Him
see Revelation 2:10
in something like a third of the World, to a degree
it's already happening
more now than ever and ever since the beginning

but wherever the laws of man don't conflict, we'll obey them
those running everything
into the ground
authorities still established by Him
and much perhaps to enact His judgment
though here and for now, slowed down
by His will and our prayers
yeah, God bless those sneaky billionaires
them and their souls sold for total control

go figure

all the money in the world can't fill a God-sized hole
hence their objective number one
yeah, drastic population reduction
#GeorgiaGuidestones
or, Agenda 21 anyone?

well, regardless, if you know it's them you can't trust
why not join THE resistance?
yeah, be a real rebel and simply follow Jesus
sure, with me, you might likely be placed on some watch-list
or worse
and if I ever die or disappear mysteriously
I won't be so surprised
He warned us of this
and in the meantime
I'm betting my life that *He is*

but believe anything but
if you insist
and you're aligned with them
just a conformist
on their team and falling for it
for centuries they've spent
painting The Way as just one of many
or anything but
and in decades most recently
with a vengeance, these efforts have been ramped up
ensuring it's with anything but God that you agree
catering to inclinations, most natural
to compete with Him too
and all of this, biblical
see psalm 2

why do the nations rage and people plot in vain?
it's 'cause those with the most
just might be beyond evil if not simply insane
conspiring together against the God of the universe
meanwhile worried most about the price of gas
most care nor notice not being led astray
led to believe our God given rights are initially issued
by the state
yeah, they giveth and taketh away
but happy enough if we can just marry the gay
while enslaved we stay
to all things Godless and pointless if not poisonous
perhaps wrapped up in whatever celebrity nonsense
if we ourselves aren't dying, trying to be famous
while never giving a second's thought to the eternity after this
turning right to the Feds in times of crisis
trained in this way to treat them
as we ought to treat the Lord Jesus
while those who vote can only hope to elect the lesser evil
sorry to say, but working with and in a rigged
and sickened system
can't fix a problem that's spiritual

I got it
let's just call what's right, wrong and wrong, right
sure
redefine all you want
meanwhile, for evil
there was, is and always will be one cure
Christ
take Him or leave it
hate Him or believe it
He loves the hell out of us
and they've cremated their care
yeah, I'm not sure they could care much less

but again
take heart
for these things must happen
and the end is not yet

J.O.Y.

ah, it's that time of year again
when we hopefully gather with some family and friends
exchange gifts and laughs and if we're fortunate enough, perhaps we gorge ourselves
yeah, and maybe throw in some pretty lights, a tree, stockings
all in good fun
for there's nothing wrong with a little keeping of tradition
or not
so long as we remember the birth of that Anointed One
the coming to earth of God's only Son
yes
and more than anything
may our joy be in Him
and may our joy in Him be complete

and happiness?
well, of course
but joy
for it lasts
as the thing about happiness is
well, it happens
yeah, it comes
and it goes
and before you know

for the happenstance of happiness
is only the result of circumstance
but in the midst of some less than blissful experience
joy's presence or absence really reveals right where we stand
upon the rock, or sand
God, or the schemes of man
so right when you think you've lived
just as much life as you can
right when you think something's got to give
read where it says God so loved us that He gave
Him
of whom, true joy is only a thought away
that is, if you know you are depraved
and He is what and who you need
as there is no other name by which any of us are saved

oh, and God, we trust you, though us you slay
as to us, You came
for upon us You have compassion
but what is man, that you are mindful of him?

and for no thing but the joy set before Him
with no thing at His disposal
He endured the cross
and He secured that very same joy for us
and it is for this that we can rejoice
always
not just on Christmas
and yeah sorry kids, but the real reason for this season
has not much of anything to do with a Santa Claus
that once mayhaps, legit historical figure
quite possibly twisted over time to further Satan's cause
averting our eyes onto any thing but our heavenly prize
getting kids to trip into that trap of chasing happiness
looking forward to temporal gifts
that is, if you've been nice
as opposed to naughty
but the thing is, everyone sins
and for which, death is the fee
oh, but the free gift of God is this
eternal life through Christ Jesus, the LORD

and thanks to His obedience
His finished work and the joy it affords
let's enjoy every un-promised day

and when everyone else complains
let's remember and give thanks
for that book of James
and for the many trials that we face
sent to test our faith
yes, pure joy
let us consider them nothing less than
knowing that they produce within us, patience

and while for You, we wait
ever since You were raised and whisked away
Christ, take Your place
in our hearts
for with You, to face the day, we know we need nothing else
yes saints, take your places
wherever you are
armed with the joy only He brings
we can joyfully embrace anything
even our extended family

vows for now

I take you
so and so
to be my
I don't know
we'll sleep together
live together
have a kid or two
and I'll be there for you
until I can't take it anymore
I get bored
or I find someone new

so, so-and-so, so long as it's mutually beneficial
according to all media, social
let's make it official
yeah, "in a relationship"
boyfriend/girlfriend
whatever you wanna call it
I don't care if the whole world knows it
we're having all the fun of marriage
you know, just minus the commitment
minus the planning and the wedding
and minus all that paperwork
yeah, what do they say?
if the milk you get from some cow is free
why buy it?
and if yours and my first time was with some girl or guy
we used to know long ago
we know there's no getting that back
so why save it?

and besides, by now
"husband and wife" sounds to me like only a formality
or just some over-priced piece of jewelry
I mean, maybe if we were gay
we'd at least have some sort of statement to make
but, so-and-so, we ain't so, why risk it?
you know, statistics would have us ending up divorced
but just like in that 50 shades
we know, no part of love should ever be restricted
or forced
so how's about we just let nature run its course

just think of it
you get to keep your last name
and I get to keep my eyes and my options open

so convenient
isn't it?
being all grown up
as for the rules, we make 'em up
yeah, who's to say we're wrong?
for if it feels good, it's right, right?
and I think we got a good thing going
so long as we both consent
that is
until your faults do us part

and on that note
you know what
on second thought
please, forget I said anything
yeah, sorry
it's just not working out

in remembrance

now, I don't know about you
or what or where you come from
but for now and like you
of all the times and places we could be
here we are

ok, call me Captain Obvious
but please, don't miss this
yes, consider the miraculous
for all previous moments
have led up to this one
even those rolled out before we were born or reborn
yes, all of them
the good, the bad and everything in between
yeah, sometimes it really seems like we're all part of a story

and again, I don't know about you
but I'm kinda dense
for over and over I'm finding
it's not that I need to be taught
it's that I need reminding
for right when I reach for that which was wrote on my heart
or so I thought
oh, how oft-forgot
yeah, how prone I am to stray
filling my own head
polluting my own soul with the nonsense
the distractions of the day
what a shame
the very Words of God get erased, replaced
with some less than innocent songs sang
by gossip and hearsay
technology and every less than beneficial thing
oh Father God, show us Your ways

what have You done?
Creator is just one of Your Names
You create
with only words
the earth, life, the light
yes, Your words are so much the Truth
You say it, and it is
poof
yeah, here's foolproof proof for the fools
we exist

and in Your divine everything
You define everything
what is good and what evil is
and You could flood the whole earth if you wanted
and You did
and every technicolor rainbow ever since
has served to remind, remind, remind us of this
and Your promise

yes, all of Your promises are yes
as seen, as sent in the person and the work of Your Son

Jesus, what have You done?
Savior is also a name of Yours
You save
as You take upon Yourself
the cross, death and sin itself
we accept this and You accept us
wretches, fully deserving Your sentence
and Your mercy extended?
with arms, long enough
we ask and you forgive us
we seek and knock and You find, open and never forget us
and lest we forget
being delivered out from our proverbial Egypts
You busted us out of deadly shackles and chains
and placed us in the heavenly places
like You and with You, raised
and all of our past accomplishments, exploits
we consider them as refuse
next to knowing You

for we were dead until with You, we died
inside of us, You said, "let there be light"
and into You, into Your life, we were baptized

and with Your Spirit, filled

and ever since and even before then
as all things are held
You have held us all together

yes, just what have you done?
the Name, LORD is Yours
You sustain
and You say who goes and who gets another day
while to die is gain anyway
but You have brought us thus far
thanks to Your providence
we are provided for
yes again, here we are
as You have pulled through over and over
and pulled us through how many a fire?
lest we forget
the answered prayers
the life-changing words and nudges
from You Yourself and from godly sisters and brothers

and even as Your former enemies
for whom You died at the right time
we can't even recall every close-call
every near-miss and tragedy averted
yes, every one, we probably deserved it
as of more than we know, we have been spared
we felt alone, but You were there
we thought we had no one, but You cared

so, here we are
in remembrance of You
living like communion
until You return or call us to You

the appraisal

you know what this world needs?
more restaurants
yeah, more cafes and coffee shops
more iced americanos, vanilla cappuccinos
double espresso mocha latte whatevers
yeah, more variations and flavors
more appetizers, entrées and desserts
and for afterwards, more bars
of all sorts
pubs and those for sports
and while we're at it
tougher, faster, stronger professional athletes
paid more
and more perceptive referees
with whom everyone agrees
and in between
funnier commercials for newer and better products and services
and more cheerleaders please
yes, more ladies
wearing less
but more clothes for us
more clothing stores
featuring the latest fashions, of course
who cares what country or conditions they were made in?
more coats, jackets, hats, bags and accessories
more flip-flops, sandals, boots and shoes
for more walking, running, working and working-out
yes, more muscle and less fat
more gyms and fitness centers
schools and learning centers
church buildings and programs
government buildings and programs
more access to a faster internet
and more virtual recognition
yeah, for me, more likes, shares, comments and friends
more pictures tagging me
and for prettier hair, nails and skin
more barber shops, spas and salons

and on TV, more reality
more celebrities and juicier gossip
more sitcoms, dramas and exposés
more charming talk shows, guests and hosts
raunchier comedians
but more of the same old actors
in bigger blockbusting movies
with side-splitting, scarier, more interesting plots
more mind-blowing video games
with endless maps, levels and mods
more concerts, festivals and parades
faster, bigger, indestructible phones
with more and more updates and upgrades
more and more apps
more plans and options
more and more ways to stay up to date
more articles and opinions
more poems and paintings and songs and books
more starving artists and authors
rappers and rockers
tattoos and parlors
drugs and booze
sex and food

yeah, do it, see it, get it, be it
over and over
go there, do that
week in, week out
weekend after weekend
until
ah, there's just nothing to do in this place
yeah, nothing to do in this city
this country
this world

that's it!
I'm not made for this world
yeah, there's got to be something
something more
worth living for

ah, there is
and His Name is King of Kings
Lord of Lords
yeah, I'm talking about Jesus
and get this

He's better than anything in this gross and bored world
and any one of us is only one
reverent and worshipful thought of Him away
from feeling and being fulfilled

therefore
whatever has and may come
fortunate or un
yes, whatever we undergo or have undergone
terrific or horrific
epic or humdrum
disease, drought, famine, war
with every reason to mourn
or while for us, a party is being thrown
yes, in every moment
there is a response, perfect
wherein lies, I'd surmise, the secret to being content

and long after some song is sung
and way before it had ever begun
yes, beyond music

worship

yes, let's worship God with our very lives
our bodies, a living sacrifice
and our minds
taken captive and made obedient to Christ

for the greatest pleasure's sake

even if we're in some discomfort or even pain
let's keep the hands of our hearts raised
for however much my flesh wants to forget Him, give in
and/or complain
my soul knows, this and every single thing was brought to fruition
brought into existence for one purpose
His praise

because God, despite perhaps popular belief
owes not one apology
though His empathy is set at 100%
He owes no one any thing
Creator, Giver and Sustainer of all things
worthy is He alone to receive all fame
for simply what and who He is
for what He'll do, what He's doing and what He did

by His will and with one Word
all of Creation was born
but against His will and with one bite
all of humanity has turned
yes, all fall short
but God
in His mercy
in His love for the whole world
He gave His only begotten Son
through whom, that veil was torn
yes, the faultless, divine Christ Jesus
He became our filthy, unmentionable sin
and He died the death we deserve upon that cross
and with that and with His being risen
the chasm between God and us is crossed
and we're just waiting now, for His return

and knowing that we know that we know this
we can and should rejoice
always
as we've been doubly blessed ever since

through faith
mistakes erased
AND declared righteous
boldly we can approach the Throne of Grace
when or where ever
no matter what direction we face
and how we work our jobs
how we embrace loss
what comes out when we open our mouths?
not what goes in, necessarily

yes, full or hungry
to share where we stand
as beggars who have found bread
in every circumstance, we have the chance
to worship God

and why would or should we?
because again, He is worthy
and the ability to do so is a gift

and if I ever brag
I brag in this
Christ has shown me just how to handle plenty or lack
in fact, how He oft talked
I'm pretty sure suffering is where it's at
I mean, how else will anyone see Him in us
unless we go through some real stuff?
as He sure did
yeah, how sure is our faith?
if it's never tested
as there and then is where and when we can really know Him
the God of Isaac and Jacob who's got our back
yeah, so, how's about we stand together in the gap?
for the orphan, the widow, the outcast and the cripple
acknowledging Him in the process
giving Him all thanks and praise and credit
everywhere, where it is due

and in Spirit
and Truth
because He is worth it
let's worship until it hurts
yes, let's worship God with all we've got
in front of this whole world
full of proud cowards coddling themselves to death
as we once were
and as we sometimes are
but we know that we know that we are now His broken conquerors
in need of Him, our Savior, as much as ever

you know what this world needs?
more of the LORD Jesus
and less me

cement to be

to the bone of my bones that is my bride
flesh of my flesh that is my wife
woman
as you are, you are the Church to my Christ

so repent
and believe
and be baptized
in this

follow me and for you
for the rest of our lives
I lay down my life
yes, it is you, I choose
so, give me your best and your worst and everything in between
and in you, beauty is all I see
only fairness and that which is altogether lovely
oh yes, and so much
as that is how He sees
us
perfected by His choice
to redeem
so, I'll sweep your sins under the rug of my love
as He does
and with the water of the Word, wash you clean

but, as is pleasing to Him, please do for me the same thing
extend to me this mercy
for I need it too
and it seems
at least as much as I could say "you're welcome"
I should probably be saying "I'm sorry"
and it's one thing to declare all of the above
it's another to show it in deed
so let's love not only in speech
and as He leads me
I'll lead
so, submit
and I am your servant King
for you, my precious Queen

oh, so strange how this exchange changes us
in ways we can't explain nor fully sense

oh, ever since
yes
the sweetest question was asked
and answered with the sweetest 'yes'
yes, it is this that begins the process
one you or I will never take back
this pact
as of me, you are a part
and I, of you
and until we really see what this reflects
when we can finally see clearly
the point of combining our lives
the point of everything

yes, until then
I'm yours, and you're mine
as cliché' as it might be
so, let's let love be genuine
yes, let's love
patiently, kindly
without envy or pride
yeah, that's the stuff
selflessly, fearlessly
forgetting what lies behind
until the day we die
together
pursuing perfection
and time and time again
we will let each other down
but no record of these wrongs can be found
as we thrive
by and while pressing onward
upward
toward the Bridegroom
He who is our love
our Heavenly Prize

all but One

humanity agrees
throughout all of history
and with a percentile around the 90's
yes
there's something
or someone out there
a he, she or it more than just math
a responsible party perhaps
for all the observable order
and larger than life itself
yes, a mind
in an otherwise chaotic universe
dare I say, an intelligence
behind the design

and I don't know about you
but it wasn't for long that I could give thanks only to time
for our being here
for sunsets and seasons
hugs and kisses, for coffee and beer
landscapes and laughter, poetry and music,
and for limited yet sufficient senses to experience it
holy moly, that something out there loves our stinking guts

c'mon, admit it
you're at least agnostic

and check out the science of fine tuning
just try to tell me that it doesn't seem
like all of reality revolves around us
not to say that we're all that or really very much
more like that capital 'S', Someone had us in thought
when setting it all up
I mean, just a little more or less of whatever element
a little closer or farther in any orbit
a little sooner or later and splat
we're all goners

and if there be a power higher
we're surely life-forms of a sort
quite a bit lower
and trying to wrap our finite minds around the whys
trying to work and earn our way to God
kinda like bacteria in a petri dish
looking up a microscope lens and trying to impress
and figure humanity out

so, if God wanted to be known
wouldn't God need to be the One?
making the effort
reaching down

just saying
of all the ways of thinking
that suppose to know anything
all are about what you do and what you have done
not about God, reaching out and stepping down
oh yeah, all ways of thinking
but One

traps

sorry
I just don't want to
yeah, I won't like to
I can't
it's just not worth it
and, and God's telling me not to
I'm sure of it
oh, decisions, decisions
with more than a single option
one could go just about insane
these days
seriously considering almost anything
just about any level of involvement or investment
so much so, that maybe next to nothing ever happens
nothing different
and you know, "I don't knows" are better off
as just plain noes
so, I let it go
this opportunity to what?
grow?
please
why risk the regret or embarrassment?
do what you want, I'll stick to what I know
yeah, until I face it and admit
man, maybe I've been missing out
maybe I've been a sort of coward
and you know what?
they say you really only regret the things you don't do
so, next time, count me in
yeah, whatever it is, I'm your dude
and now
with cleared eyes stricken near-sighted
still beautiful feet stumble upon something
of beauty
promising
and with so little resisting
but making light of the mystery
foolish flesh fills in the gaps
making the unknown winsome
even yellow and red flags

wait, is that you, wisdom?
screaming bloody murder
just warranted warnings going unheeded
making wishy-washy before rushing in
as wants wear the same uniforms as what's needed
oh, decisions, decisions
shut up, wisdom
let your I guesses be yeses
and your I don't knows be no more
don't you know?
hesitation is cowardice
and decisiveness?
divine
just give it time
wishes arise
wishing to rewind
and going over and over it
never going to be over it
when it's at all times, in mind
yeah, if only I had turned right instead of left
but at the time
left felt so right
despite the signs
yeah, it must have been that worst enemy of mine
you know, me, myself, I and my seemingly immortal--
yeah, why won't you freaking die, pride?
regardless, now, paying the price
just letting yeses be yeses
feeling sidelined
mixed up in messes disguised as blessings
now
rifling through the lies
AND the laughs
yeah, despite the eggshells and all that broken glass
man, so green was that grass
but there's no going back
so I'll look beyond all of this
and I'll plot, plan and project
and I'll store and save all of my best
for the whatever's next

yeah, you know this too shall pass
I just hope it does so, and fast
but this too, is a trap
because these numbered days
yeah, they don't last
and I'll soon regret not having made more
of every day that has elapsed
as they are as good as I let them be
and one at a time is the only way these days can be taken
so, now I see
thinking too critically of something
OR too highly
yeah, making much of nothing
OR not enough
of would-be, should-be deal-breakers
and fixed on the future
plotting and planning what is far from sure
OR planted in the past
yeah, always looking forward
OR back
all of these are traps
so much so that being present
being really aware of this fleeting moment
kind of like a balancing act
while the whole world teems with things to distract
and get us all up into, what?
missing out, on just about all we've got
you know, now
and each other
and being bogged and dragged down
by nothing of which to be proud
oh God
You've got me, yeah?
I see, this is where and when I am at
and You have pulled me up and out from every trap
yes, all along
You have had my back
and with that
You can have all of me
now and from here on out

the chief of sins

so, there's this guy
we'll call him Pride
sure, he might look pretty alright
on the outside
but behind the smile
Pride's not long or often satisfied
as only his wants, needs and opinions are bona-fide
and always competing and comparing
something to criticize, he always finds
and so easy to bother
from inside, Pride whines and cries
"I deserve more and better!"

but Pride, you can never advise
for he is always right in his own eyes
yeah, Pride knows best, no matter what
"hey, I got this
I don't need that
and besides, it won't work"

yeah, don't be surprised when Pride lashes out
against all things wise
or when called out
so easily offended
Pride can't stand being corrected
as he's always on the defensive
for all Pride sees are flaws
but none of his own

"yeah, this or that or they are what's wrong
it or they need to change
yeah, if only this or that were different
and if only they were a little more this or that"

Pride cannot love
any but himself
thinking nothing of or for anyone else
and on his own way, he insists
for any love sent his way is just not enough
and Pride lies
as there are no temptations that he resists
while himself, he justifies
and never willing to apologize

but, to Pride, I am mostly blind
for he hides
yeah, to survive, he'll sometimes twist and writhe
until he looks something like self-pity
whatever it takes to not submit to any authority
yeah, whether trying hard to be recognized
OR to himself, confined
still Pride
this pitiful kind is just kinda disguised as the good guy
Pride's adversary, Humility
just beginning to be exhibited
the moment I simply admit it

oh, how often
I'm that guy
yeah, my problem is pride
and when I don't think so
pride really is my problem
all the more so
because Pride is in denial
as deception is very much his style

so, Pride, die
for I see
to be strong, I must first realize
I'm weak
and to be wise, I must first admit my folly
and so Humility can come to life
here, I'll put Pride to death already

but what's Humility like?
well, despite his smile
he might actually look a little ugly
but give Humility just a little while
and he'll prove himself, every time
for he satisfies
always
always giving thanks
he just doesn't lose his cool
Humility is confident and kind
he says, "hi"
"how are you?"
and with care, maybe even a prayer
he gives an answer
Humility makes the most of every moment
so easy to please and teach
any grief leads him to repent
he doesn't know it all, and he knows it
yeah, Humility can take a hint
or a hit
knowing those hurting others, are hurting
themselves
so, taking on the form of a servant
Humility is loved and loves
and next to him, he considers others to be more important

and if I go on describing Humility much more
I'll be straight up, describing Jesus Christ
the LORD
for what greater demonstration of humility is there?
none, of which any one is or every will be aware
for God himself took on flesh
and for all of us, He took on death
and pride is just one of our sins for which He died
but it's from pride that every sin is derived
and if there was just one sin that kept anyone from God
and His blessings
including eternity with Him
and if there was just one sin
preventing God's children from becoming godly
holy moly, it's pride
for without mind, Pride speaks
and he says, "I'm fine"
meanwhile
Humility sees his need
and the Truth, he seeks
and by God, Humility is found
because my God gives grace to the humble
and He opposes the proud

so maybe now's about the time to get on my knees
to give thanks for not being like others?
no
but like this
please God, be merciful to me
the chief of sinners

Pharisaical disbelief

look
yeah, just look around at all the churches in this town
of all the denominations, variations and divisions
bible studies, commentaries and translations
on the outside, looking in
one may wonder
"God in heaven, just which Jesus am I supposed to believe in?"
and like that
yeah, even as a sweet baby
Jesus so often gets flushed
out with the bathwater that is one's concept of "religion"

oh, the irony
considering those who were so openly christened by Christ
as blind-guides
fools
white-washed tombs
serpents
vipers
hypocrites

these are the religious
yay, for ye are as unmarked graves
trampled by the multitudes unaware
made all the more unclean by your rotting remains
six feet underfoot if not under car

yes, these are the ones whom He condemns
for He simply wants our hearts

not empty, loveless works
no godless ambition
for all of this is fuel for what?
every division
between all of us
living contrary to the true doctrine
that we've learned
and must re-learn
Jesus
The One
good enough for dudes in prison
but not public schools and America's children
and what about us?
are we gonna wait til we hit rock bottom?
are we gonna wait til it's too late before looking up?
yes, just when will we open our wooden eyes
and rock hard hearts?
without God
yes, without Christ
we've got nothing
we are poor, sick, wicked and cripple
in need of God
in need of Jesus
who chastised no one like He did those
those confusing themselves for righteous
healthy and/or rich
apart from Him
never a part of Him
while wherever He is, is Heaven

to Oslo (the dwarf hotot)

you fear what you don't know
have no fear

I raise you up
twirl you around
and put you down
have no fear

I have you
and every thing you have
I gave
yes, every little piece of food that makes its way
oh, into your fluffy little face
my, that's a pretty B.A. cage
and you've seen only a fraction of this place
yeah, to you, I'm kinda like God
you see?
for you, I paid
yes you, I saved
so, fear not

and now, be calm and hold on
as I hold you close
trust me and enjoy me
and within my reach, happily stay

or revolt
do your own thing
and to where ever you think you can hide
run scared

oh, don't make me think of you as just another impulse buy
I would never
you adorable thing
and besides, I find you every time

so, fear not
but fear me
love me
and know me
yes, know, I have control where you don't
and I could crush or rip you apart
but I won't
I chose you
now you, I have
and you, I love
so, be happy and wise and brave

an only

there is no one else
no one, I would rather trust
oh, with all of my love
all of my everything
all of me
and yes, I must
but this is not the because
why you and I are we
and you and me will always be
always us
so let's look at all back and know, feel and see
together
we have been through so, so much
and God's been so, so good to us
though we know, in the all-too-soon future
we'll go through much more
and whatever it is
God forbid us to forget
as the troubles of tomorrow come around
with every morning comes new mercy
and may we, joyful be
as we acknowledge Him, our greatest need
yes, let's realize the ever-present feast
all of God's blessings
all of His bountiful dealings
with us
oh, and with me
out of everything
there is nothing else
no thing in life more precious
than you to me
and long after beauty and youth flee
we'll still have us
and this trust
oh, how I crave every hour, every day
your love
your touch
your everything
you, truly
and me, I'm yours truly
as long as we breathe
and as long as you will just have me

at peace in war

in this life
this sort of game
sometimes
there's only one way to win
only one thing to do
yeah, and that's to lose
and usually
there's really only one way out
and that's through
and always
there's only one escape from the weight of every lie
and that's speaking the truth
but like learning a new language
first, we must hear it

and mattering more than the battles we lose
is how good we are at losing
yeah, just how good are we at going through?
and speaking the truth?

but when relating is like road rage
drive straight
do not retaliate
do not wave
do not cut or flip them off
let it go
it's gonna be okay
it's not worth it
you know, many have died that way

oh but, what to say, what to say
when whatever you say or do
stands accused
of being the fire
to only innocent fuel
the walking, breathing, talking contention in the room
with any and every excuse
as attractive as repellent
as affectionate as a nuke
the only thing to do
is be silent
the only thing to say
is nothing
until hearing something different
something honestly desperate
like 'sorry'
and until then
there's only one way to break free
somewhere
come clean
and everywhere
simply remember
what you believe

unintentionability

listen
we need to talk
about us
you and me
yeah, how are we doing?
better?
or is worse what we are getting?
are we giving in more and more?
more or less?
giving into the world, the devil, our flesh?
how are we giving of ourselves at all?

yeah, when we're alone, together
are we at our best?
or something else?
our worst, perhaps?
yeah, how much do we like ourselves?
how much do we love, enjoy and respect each other?
can we gracefully give and receive correction?
or are we just enabling one another?
are we doing things no one knows?
keeping many things between only us?
things of which we'd be embarrassed, scared, or pissed
oh, if anyone knew
anyone, but us
oh yeah, and God

remember Him?
what does He think?
yeah, what do we think He thinks, about us?
do we want what He wants?
is He our greatest love, joy and hope?
what, for us, does He hope?

what has He said for, to and about us?
well, what does He say?
yeah, what is He saying, to us?
what is He doing?
what is it that He did?
are we remaining watchful?
listening?

what's this?
oh, let's just watch and listen
to a little of the latest
something funny
something foreign
some more of one more band or artist
or even something serious

tragic

whatever

this blessed test

enough is enough
except for when it's not
yeah, never really alright
despite getting what you want
over and over
and even if and when you call every shot
over and over
forever stumbling over something
you know not what
and at best, feeling just a little less than completely empty
starving though stuffed up on.. you name it

come on, you know what it is that you need
or at least I do
sure, call me arrogant
but I've tasted and I've seen
this whole world's got nothing on the One who made it
and eventually, everyone will see
but for now, hidden only to those who don't seek
wholeheartedly

so how about now?
come on, sit
have a think
a drink
from these words, the Word like water
living and active
yeah, gold and silver
I do not have
but something infinitely greater, I give
yes, in the name of Jesus Christ of Nazareth
LIVE

pick up your mat, your crap and walk
everyday, pick up your cross
and let the scales continually fall from your eyes
Jesus is the Truth
so, what does that make any other worldview?
lies
and if Jesus is the way and the life
any other way of life must be what?
a waste of time

so, sleeper, arise
and be still
and know
God is God
and you are not
and His grace is enough
especially when you don't get what you want
and when you realize that you don't call the shots
yeah, let go already and let God
let go of all of your struggling to make it work
leave room for Him to make it right
open up
walk in the light
and let Him heal your every hurt

He knows and He cares and for us
He's been through much, much worse
and if we really know this
yeah, if we really know Him
we know, this too shall pass
this momentary light affliction
whatever pitifully first-world problem
or even some big as-far-as-we're-concerned burden
yes, even tragedy pales in comparison
for anything we could think to complain about now
won't be worth a thought in heaven

but until then
on the altar of fill-in-the-blank
the life He gave and died to save goes to waste
looking for more than a little relief
a means to escape
the mundane
all the monotonous stuff seemingly in the way
this is the very cross we have to carry, everyday
the who, what or where we just can't change
this is precisely what God would have us go through
who He'd have us bear with
and with a smile on our heart's face
yeah, with this faith we can't fake
us with God, even this whole world can't shake

yeah, isn't it great?
any time or place
the more aware of Him that we are
the more we are armed, with His grace
and fitted with the Spirit by which He was raised
yes, ours is the choice
oh, to be annoyed
or to enjoy
any and every one and thing
for His sake and glory
and for our good and that of the whole world
may Him and His Kingdom be what we truly seek
and let's really be the change that He wants to see

The Most Cool

forget all the t-shirts
bumper stickers
tattoos and necklaces
and all those Christian pop songs
trying desperately to sound good and cool

Jesus IS really good and scary cool
yeah like, Sammy Davis freaking Jr. got nothing on Him, cool
like wearing shades
popped collar and rockin' the saxophone times a billion, cool

cause get this
even suffering through the worst injustice
first, ironically if not preposterously
arrested and put on trial for what?
blasphemy
because the religious Pharisees got
that Jesus was equating Himself with God
His silence pleading guilty for Him
and mocked
spat upon
flogged
that is whipped and beaten within an inch of death
yes, and all the way to the cross
crown of thorns and all
long and thick nails pounded through His wrists and ankles
slammed into the ground
and on some wine for the pain
He passed
and not once, did He whine, complain or even protest

"forgive them for they know not what they do"
yeah, THAT IS COOL

and besides willingly going through hell
where is He?

134

well, He's chillin' with the woman at the well
He's hanging with the world's rejected and unwanted
lepers, tax collectors, shepherds
as far as the world and they themselves are concerned
the really uncool
yeah, He's loving the otherwise unlovable
and He's calming the storm
He's overturning tables at the greedy and twisted temple
He's opening the eyes of the blind
and man, He even weeps when it's right
yeah, He is THAT cool

so, what about you?
yeah, when something, anything takes an extra minute or two
ooh, or when the stylist goofs up your hair-do
or how about when you gotta do something
something you just don't want to
and what if all your plans seem to fall through
and all hell breaks loose
are you cool?
or do you lose your poop?
yeah, how's your 'tude?
are you cool with the Truth?
or do you hear a thing you didn't think and blow a fuse?
anything disagreeing with you, does it just not compute?
even right now, what's your mood?
again, are you cool?
cool, like Jesus?

only the hurt and confused, hurt and confuse
has He made you immune?
or does the world still got you hurt and confused too?
soften, open, look and give up
let Him have and heal you
He'll make you cool with whatever
whatever you've gone, are going or are going to go through
through hell perhaps, all the way to heaven
whatever momentary light affliction
all the while, pointing others to Him and helping them too

but until then
can you stand solitude?
how about silence?
such was His refuge
away from the busyness
being busy about the Father's business
He'd lose sleep to just with God, commune
would I? would you?
such is where He tells us to go
from mountaintops into prayer closets
us of His
made anew
and made cool with the Truth and unto death
by, with and like God in the flesh
the coolest dude ever, Jesus

I was born in Canton, Ohio where I lived with my parents and older brother for the first 12 years of life. For two years after that, we lived in Mt. Pleasant, Michigan before finally settling in Fort Wayne, Indiana where I've lived for most of my life and where, in my 25th year, I came to believe and trust in the God of the Bible. By then, I had already been writing and reciting poetry publically for about 7 years, and since then, you can probably tell what inspires me more than anything. Around that same time, I graduated with a bachelor's in interpersonal communications and mass media communications with a minor in public relations. About 5 years later, I married my lovely and beautiful wife Kayla, with whom the adventures never stop. Eight months in, we were in Cheongju, South Korea where I taught English for a year before returning to Fort Wayne. As I'm finishing up this book, we are about a month away from moving to Greenville, South Carolina as I'm transferring jobs with a reputable plasma donation center.

>Thank you again for reading.
>I praise and thank God for you.
>May He always bless you and keep you.

>>With His Love,
>>Adam J. Bodnar
>>email: adambpoetry@gmail.com
>>artist page: facebook.com/adambpoetry

Made in the USA
Columbia, SC
01 February 2018